Build It Right

Supervising the Construction of Your Home

Kenneth L. Petrocelly

To the unenlightened
who went before us
and paid the price

Build It Right

Supervising the Construction of Your Home

Kenneth L. Petrocelly

TAB BOOKS
Blue Ridge Summit, PA

FIRST EDITION
FIRST PRINTING

Copyright © 1990 by TAB BOOKS
Printed in the United States of America

Library of Congress Cataloging-in-Publication Data

Petrocelly, K. L. (Kenneth Lee), 1946-
Build it right : supervising the construction of your home / by
Kenneth L. Petrocelly.
p.   cm.
ISBN 0-8306-7433-0 — ISBN 0-8306-3433-9 (pbk.)
1. House construction. 2. Building—Superintendence.   I. Title.
TH4812.P48   1990
690'.837—dc20   89-48457
                                                                           CIP

TAB BOOKS offers software for
sale. For information and a catalog,
please contact TAB Software Department,
Blue Ridge Summit, PA 17294-0850.

Questions regarding the content of this book
should be addressed to:

Reader Inquiry Branch
TAB BOOKS
Blue Ridge Summit, PA 17294-0214

Acquisitions Editor: Kimberly Tabor
Book Editor: Susan L. Rockwell
Production: Katherine Brown

Contents

Introduction

AS THOSE OF US PAST 40 KNOW, THE ERA OF THE CRAFTSMAN IS OVER. NOT SO you say? When's the last time you had your shoes resoled by a cobbler? What's a cooper? Where's the cabinetmakers' shop in your town? Who do you call to . . . ? Let's face it, unless it can be cooked in a minute, ready in an instant, or served in a flash, people don't want it. We live in a hurry up, get it over with society and would rather buy anew than fix the old. Every facet of our lives has been affected by the pursuit of the quick, almighty dollar. The builder's chant is get up, get in, get done, and get gone. In the construction arena, labor takes time, time equates to money, and money is the name of the game. To make a profit in today's competitive market, builders are often forced to become creative in keeping their expenses down. There is a high cost associated with cheap construction. If you cut corners on your home, all you'll end up with is a round house.

This book was written for those of us who remain committed to the American dream of building and owning our homes but want to forgo the nightmare of being taken to the bank while pursuing it. It's a user's manual for persons unfamiliar with the home-building process, a refresher course in customer communications for the builder, and a handy reference for anyone contemplating a construction project, however small. Its text alerts prospective owners to the rigors of project work and warns them of the consequences associated with poor workmanship, cheap construction, and haste.

The manner in which this message is delivered is intended to be instructional and entertaining. A laid back style takes you step-by-step through the home building jungle with nary a scratch, as though the author were walking you through it in person—machete in hand. But don't let the novel approach fool you; if properly heeded, the information this book contains could save you hundreds or even thousands of dollars and ensure the success of virtually any construction project you might undertake.

1

What? Me Worry?

IT'S BEEN SAID THAT PHYSICIANS BURY THEIR MISTAKES AND THAT GOOD cooks eat theirs, but have you ever wondered what becomes of the blunders builders make? Simply put, they hide them; cover up—in the true sense of the term. Now that's not to say that all building contractors are crooked or out to take advantage of the masses. On the contrary, it's been my experience that just the opposite is true. I firmly believe that most contractors are qualified and at least initially intend to provide a solid product. So what's my point? Even if you're dealing with a builder whose reputation is above reproach, who employs only highly skilled craftsmen and uses "nothing but the best" in materials, mistakes will occur more frequently than you might suspect. Take for example this random sampling of construction glitches I witnessed recently close to where I live. They are from unrelated projects and belong to different builders.

HIDDEN BLUNDERS

These pictures reveal some of the defects that the new owners will be living with but might never become aware of. Figure 1-1 shows a portion of a *sole plate*, the horizontal member of a studded wall that attaches it to the floor. (In this case the appliance wall of a kitchen.) Instead of it being run continuously, forming the full length of the wall, it was pieced together. This lack of continuity can have an adverse effect on the structural integrity of the wall when exposed to lateral forces. How's that?

Fig. 1-1. Noncontinuous sole plate located in an interior (inferior) wall.

Oh, I'm sorry. You're right; if you knew all these terms you wouldn't need to read this book. *Lateral forces* are forces that act horizontally against objects, such as the wind against a window or pressure from soil heaped against a foundation wall. A significant lateral force could be applied to this particular wall by aggressively rolling a refrigerator into place against it. I wonder if that's why people clean behind them so infrequently.

In Fig. 1-2 it's the opposite end where the problem lies. Like the sole plate, the *top plate* is a horizontal member used for forming and stabilizing framed walls. It is located at the top of vertical studs and should also be run continuously, the full length of the wall. As you can see in the illustration, such is not the case here. The plate was extended by tacking a block of wood to a joist overhead and another to a plank furred to an exterior concrete block wall. Structurally, this construction is about as sound as the one in our first example. Don't lean against the wall, guys! For sure, I wouldn't hang too heavy a cupboard on it. Moreover, the top plate shown in the example is comprised of a single 2-×-4 stud. Normally it would be laminated to a second stud of equal length called a *cap plate* or doubler, which is missing here.

A *lintel* is a horizontal member supporting the load above a window, doorway, or other opening in a wall. Depending on the application, it can be made of metal, plastic, or a number of other materials. In Fig. 1-3, the lintels used over the door frames, which appear fine, were manufactured from cast concrete. So what's the problem? It's in the positioning

Fig. 1-2. Undoubled (unstable) top plate located in an interior wall.

Fig. 1-3. Precast lintel installed too high to meet door frame.

of the lintels over the doorways. The one pictured on the right has been installed properly, the one on the left has not; unless of course the builder was considering installing a transom there. Well, he wasn't! Doors and windows in wall openings should be tied to the lintels above them in order to provide additional support to their frames. Lintels sometimes do double duty as headers, such as above the door on the right. As for the door on the left, if it isn't slammed too hard, too often . . .

POOR WORKMANSHIP

Admittedly, as investigative reporters go, I'm no Geraldo, but check this out. On a bad job you might be buying more than just poor workmanship; you might also be receiving inferior grade materials. The roofer responsible for the work represented in these four snapshots should have his scaffolding confiscated. No, the beams of light entering through the roof in Fig. 1-4 are not God's blessings on a new abode, rather it's light pouring in from the outside through knotholes, cracks, and excessive separations in and between the wood planking used to construct the roof. Figures 1-5 through 1-7 show the inferior quality of the wood used on this job and the poor workmanship shown by a mechanic who nailed the felt paper to the roof. Why he didn't fall into the building is beyond me.

Fig. 1-4. Wooden roof planks spaced too far apart.

Fig. 1-5. Inferior lumber found in the project stockpile.

Fig. 1-6. Inferior lumber installed as roof sheathing.

Fig. 1-7. Poor workmanship used to install roof felts.

BLATANT ERRORS

By no means are construction errors limited to those that can be hidden, such as pipes running through air ducts or air ducts running through beams. Some are more obvious like bathrooms lacking exhaust fans or appliances lacking headroom. Beyond these lie the SNAFU's such as those depicted in Figs. 1-8 and 1-9, which speak for themselves. Before you ask, SNAFU is an acronym used in military parlance for *Situation Normal All Fouled Up*—at least that's a close analogy.

THE CONSEQUENCES

Covering up mistakes is the most common and least expensive option to builders. If blunders are allowed to go by the board during the building process, the contractor will save money up front, but you will spend more over the long haul. There is a high cost associated with cheap construction. As a result, houses usually look better than they are built—get what you pay for.

CASE STUDIES

If you want to learn before you're burned, there's no substitute for reviewing the experiences of others who attempted the same endeavor.

Fig. 1-8. Poor coordination between concrete and water line installers.

Fig. 1-9. Newly planted trees impede pedestrian traffic along newly installed walk.

Here are three factuals I recently gleaned from a Sunday newspaper supplement covering the subject of home building with some local citizens. I refer to the articles as *The Good, Not Bad,* and *The Ugly.* Their story lines are intact; the names were changed to protect the innocent . . . dum, duh, dum, dum.

The Good

For Bob and Carol Owner, the year they spent finding a builder for their custom house was time well spent. The couple had some apprehensions about builders, so they checked around. They went to three different banks and checked with most of the home builders in the county. They rejected one after learning they wouldn't be able to visit the home site during construction. They heard complaints about other builders from the newspapers and from people they talked to. Finally, they settled on Well Built Homes Co. in Inverness to build the $70,000 house, and, so far, things look good. "We've had no problems," said Bob, a 38-year-old mining foreman, as he gave a tour through the maze of 2×4s that soon will be a three-bedroom, two-bathroom home. "The main problems are in," he said. "All the walls are where we want them."

Like most people who have houses built in Citrus County, things are going smoothly for the Owners. Only in a small minority of cases do things go wrong, and the couple said they looked long and hard to prevent that. They expect the home to be finished by March, and say it's a little ahead of schedule. The couple, originally from Poughkeepsie, NY, said they've wanted to design and build a house for years. They moved to Floral City about six years ago with their two children, Ted, 7, and Alice, 4. "This is Alice's here," said Bob, pointing proudly to what will soon be a bedroom.

The couple added several personal touches to the house they designed. "I work evenings," Bob said, so the house will have a central intercom-stereo-security system with a speaker at the front door. The breakfast nook was something they've always wanted, too. They said the builder has been receptive to the changes they've made and understanding of their fears. "We'd seen what some people had gone through," Carol Owner said. "We went to Well Built and told them what our fears were, and we checked out a couple of houses they'd built," she said. "He works with you". Many members of the building industry say they welcome such investigations before customers choose. Most builders are reputable and have nothing to hide, they say. Only in a few cases do problems arise, and often they could be avoided by a careful check in advance.

The president of the Citrus County Builders Association says a reputable builder will provide a list of customers and subcontractors. Check with the Builders Association and with the county building department. "That dream house is available to everybody," she said. "But when you get three bids on a floor plan and one is $10,000 less than the others, then take a close look before signing." For the Owners and hundreds of other people who build houses in Citrus County each year, her advice works. The Owners are renting a house near their home site, which they visit frequently. They've made minor changes as work has progressed. But now, said Carol Owner, "my concerns are picking the right colors."

Not Bad

When Paul Renter and his wife, Paula, retired from their jobs in Illinois and began searching for a retirement home, they were looking for the warmth of Florida but not the prices of some of the more populated retirement havens. They searched the Fort Myers area and found the summer heat too extreme for their liking. Orlando was too congested, and housing costs were high compared with other areas. That's why they, like thousands before them, settled in Hernando County. "Housing is considerably less," said Renter, who left the Chicago suburb of Morton Grove. "Land costs are lower, and I just like the area. We were used to the big city, and we don't miss it. This is close enough to Tampa and St. Petersburg, but you don't have the problems they do." Renter, 61, who owned a service station in Illinois, said he and his wife hired a builder to construct a three-bedroom home for them in Rainbow Woods, a Spring Hill subdivision. They moved in nine months ago. "I like the Spring Hill area," Renter said. "We're probably missing out on some conveniences, but soon enough I think we'll find these things coming this way."

Home builders say the retirees such as the Renters, who have helped make Hernando one of the fastest-growing counties in the country, are still coming. "They get a lot more house, a lot more for the deal in Hernando County than possibly anywhere else in the state," said the director of sales for Monarch Homes in Hernando County Inc. "I think the motivation is still the deal. People are getting a good deal when they come to Hernando County."

Typical new residents in Hernando County are retirees from the Midwest and the Northeast. Usually they sell their homes, get rid of their old furniture and come to Florida to live off their pensions and investments. "Most of them have the attitude that if they can go first class, they will, because if they don't, their heirs will," said a sales associate for U.S. Home at Timber Pines, a Spring Hill subdivision.

Dotty Buygood, 73, represents a variation on the typical retiree coming to Hernando County. In December, she moved into her Seven Hills home after selling a previous retirement home in Kenneth City, near St.

Petersburg. Her husband died three and a half years ago, and her mother passed away a year and a half ago. She wanted to move to a better house and get away from the memories and increasing traffic problems in Pinellas County. She loves her new house with its cathedral ceilings and color-coordinated decor. She is just a few blocks from a grocery store, which is important to her. "It's fairly easy to get to the shopping center," she said, but admits she still uses a map to find it. "And we've got a hospital nearby, and the YMCA is going to open soon." She still has to unpack a few boxes and find a doctor, eye doctor, and dentist, but otherwise Mrs. Buygood said she has settled in and enjoys the Spring Hill area. Her son, William, 40, who is a computer programmer, lives with her. They looked at quite a few areas before deciding to move to Spring Hill. "We seemed to like this the best," Mrs. Buygood said, "it was open and quiet. You feel like you can get out and spread your arms without touching the person next door."

The Ugly

Sometimes the Florida dream goes bad. It happened to Joseph Schmo and his wife, Josephine. The Edison, NJ, couple had planned for 15 years to retire to Florida and build their dream house. But before construction on their home began, Mrs. Schmo became terminally ill with lung cancer. Schmo, an electrician, had to retire early to care for her. He hoped to have their home built before his wife died so they could spend at least a little time in the sunshine. After numerous trips to Florida and a lengthy investigation of home builders, he signed a contract in November 1987 and put down $10,000 for a three-bedroom, two-bathroom home. To build their home, Schmo chose the Dambad Corporation. Amid radiation and chemotherapy treatments for his wife, Schmo kept in touch with the Dambad representatives by telephone.

In December 1987, they told him the first phase of construction on the $56,000 home was complete and asked him to send another $10,000 for the second phase. Schmo, now 61, arrived with his wife in Florida on January 12, 1988. On his property, he found a concrete slab with some rough plumbing. When he went to Dambad's office, he found a note on the door with a lawyer's phone number. He called and learned that the company was going to file for bankruptcy.

On February 2, a little more than two weeks after arriving in Florida, his wife died. In the midst of her illness, Schmo had tried to find out what had happened to his house. He went to the state attorney's office and the county building department, and he hired a lawyer. The bad news filtered out. Dambad Corporation had left dozens of incomplete homes when it closed its doors. The company filed for bankruptcy in federal court in Jacksonville in February 1988.

County officials estimate Dambad left dozens of people with incomplete homes and owed customers and subcontractors more than $400,000. Two owners of the corporation were later charged with issuing worthless checks. They were sentenced to probation and ordered to pay back thousands of dollars, but were not judged guilty of felony violations. They also face disciplinary action from the Department of Professional Regulation after admitting misconduct at a hearing January 12.

A widower with a healthy chunk of his savings gone, Schmo decided to finish the house himself. "I figured, what the hell? I'm out 25 grand," he said. "So I came back and got started." He completed much of the work himself and hired subcontractors for the rest. He finished the home in ten weeks.

A year after the nightmare, things are looking up. Schmo has a beautiful home with room for visits from his four children and seven grandchildren. He plans to remarry soon. "I'm happy with it," he said of his finished house. But he carries the bitter memories of his struggle with Dambad, and one lien on the home from a subcontractor remains. He had to pay the impact fee charged by the county, more than $1,000, twice. He originally paid it to Dambad. The company had signed a promissory note agreeing to pay the fee to the county later. "Nothing was paid," he said. "The surveyor hadn't been paid, and I had to pay to have the well drilled again." A county task force created after the Dambad problems surfaced has since persuaded the county commission to discontinue the impact fee IOUs.

Schmo said he didn't choose his builder lightly. "He was building what I thought were the best homes in Citrus County," he said. And he talked to several satisfied customers before making the decision.

One mistake, he said recently, was staying in New Jersey while construction began. "I could have saved myself $10,000 if I were here." Instead, he says he lost more than $20,000. He was lucky that he was able to finish the home himself. "I feel sorry for people that have no construction background whatsoever," he said. His advice to others up North who might be following the Florida retirement dream: "Do not build unless you can be here." From 1,000 miles away, he said, "you've got no way of knowing if what the guy's telling you is true or not true."

2

Dissecting a Project

THE PROCESS OF HAVING A HOUSE BUILT IS VERY MUCH LIKE CLIMBING A staircase whose steps are numbered, beginning from one, at its base and increasing sequentially until its upper landing is reached. Whereas the stairs can be travelled in a number of fashions, the order in which the steps are taken, though important, isn't as relevant as the fact that all the steps must be traversed. While outlining this chapter, I was mentally up and down those stairs so often my brain gets a charley horse every time I think about it. Here's the staircase; I recommend you proceed one step at a time. I'll post a list of questions for you to ponder on each of its risers to aid your thinking process.

ASSESSING THE ALTERNATIVES

Obviously, there are two options available to anyone searching for a place in which to live—renting or owning. Each has its satisfactions and its drawbacks. Generally speaking, renters simply pay a periodic fee for the privilege of occupying a structure but are not obligated to maintain or repair it. They are often restricted as to what they are allowed to modify within the structure, and how it can be used. Renters are not eligible for certain residential-based tax breaks afforded by the government. Home-owners, on the other hand, enjoy total freedom to use their homes in any way they choose; society norms and zoning ordinances aside. Home-owners must pay property taxes and are liable for injuries to people that occur on their property.

Fig. 2-1A. Handy man special.

Fig. 2-1B. Maintenance-free home. COURTESY OF THE SQUARE D COMPANY.

Assuming that you've weighed all the pros and cons of these options and have decided that ownership is for you, there's still a choice you must make. Will you buy an existing structure or have one built to your specifications? Once again there are advantages and disadvantages attached to both decisions. Should you decide to buy an existing one, you will be acquiring the beauty, craftsmanship, and materials of the era in which the building was constructed but also inherit the headaches caused by age, wear, and neglect. If instead you build, what you're purchasing is abstract; an idea or concept based on your perception, efforts of your builder, and outlay of your money. The result can run the gamut of dream fulfillment to nightmare. So what will it be? Before you decide, ask yourself . . .

Considerations

- What can you afford?
- What do family members think?
- Is the location right for you?
- Will the property appreciate? Depreciate?
- How will the change of seasons affect you?
- Do you mind being interrupted at work?
- How competent a handyman are you?
- Where will you live if and while you build?
- Will transportation be a factor?
- Who will your neighbors be?
- Did you consider unforeseen expenses?
- What is the present worth of the property?
- Are you sure you want to move?
- How long do you intend to live there?
- Will you have time to oversee a project?

BUYING THE RIGHT LOT

So, you've decided to build—good for you. This should prove to be the most personally gratifying, yet time-consuming, project you'll ever undertake in your lifetime. Let's go out and look for a parcel of land. Your primary concern at this point should be to focus on the general area where you want to live. North of the city you say? Okay, but why? I see. Yes, the homes are quite nice up that way; the schools are known for their academic excellence; and development is definitely progressive—all good reasons. So, where do we go to look for land? There are basically three sources: individual landowners, the government, and land investors such as developers or builders. But before you check out the legal plats in the municipal building or start talking turkey with the realtor handling the property . . .

Fig. 2-2. Relatively easy-to-clear shallow grade lot.

Considerations

- Are the houses surrounding the property in the price range in which you want to build?
- Is the land located in a subdivision having covenants or deed restrictions? What are they?
- Will the lot be large enough for expansion in the future? Too large to maintain?
- Is the land in a flood plain or subject to subsidence?
- Has the land been zoned strictly for single family dwellings?
- Is the land surrounding the lot suitable for home building?
- Has a title search been performed? What were the findings?
- Are public water and sewage lines accessible? Has a percolation test and/or soil analysis been performed?
- Is the area considered safe? Is it quiet? How close to traffic?
- Does the lay of the land support storm water run-off? Is the slope conducive to running a sewer line?
- Are nearby utilities run underground or overhead?
- Will you be required to install any sidewalk and curbing?
- Has a survey been recently performed? How much will one cost?
- How much will a title insurance policy cost me?
- Is the cost in line with comparable properties?

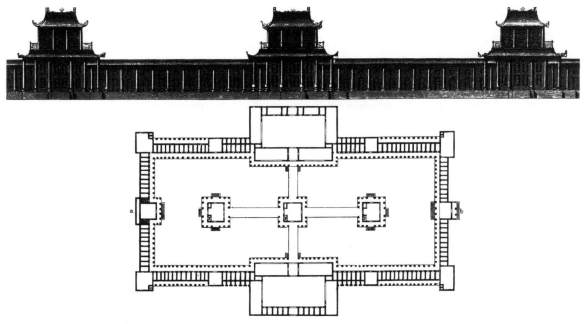

Fig. 2-3. Chinese Pagoda.

CHOOSING A DESIGN

Most often, this phase of the process is accomplished concomitantly with the hiring of your building contractor. Not that house plans can't be acquired from other sources such as architects, professional designers, or even plan books, but the drawings supplied by the builder are the ones he best understands. Subsequently, they are the ones he will feel most comfortable with when they are modified to conform to your preferences and purse. Wherever you get your plans, don't forget to ask . . .

Considerations

- Is the plan one of a kind or rubber stamped?
- Does the plan come with written specifications?
- Do the specifications include schedules and details for doors, windows, cabinetry . . . etc.?
- Is the design proven? Is it relatively easy to build?
- How much would the completed project run? Can it be modified and still retain its integrity?
- Has a model been built that you can tour? Are there similar, less expensive houses you can see?
- How good are you at visualizing abstractly?

- Does the exterior fit in with the houses in the neighborhood?
- How many square feet of living space does it contain? What is the cost per square foot?
- Does the design fit your lifestyle? How much will it cost to maintain?
- Are the rooms large enough? Does the layout provide a good traffic flow?
- Will you be supplied with copies of the plans for the bank, inspector, etc.?
- Is the design energy efficient?

Fig. 2-4. Builder's construction trailer.

HIRING A BUILDER

Hooking up with a builder is very much like making friends in the military during times of war. Generally you're only together for about a one-year hitch, but it seems like a lifetime. You end up knowing each others' darkest secrets and innermost feelings, hoping the information doesn't somehow get around. You wonder if one or both of you will come out of the miserable experience alive. This is one relationship you should consider very seriously before entering into it; a divorce midway through this marriage can literally wipe you out financially. Don't think about signing on with someone unless you answer . . .

Considerations

- Did you get at least three bids on the project? Were the builders bidding on identical plans?
- How long have the builders been in business? How reputable are they?
- Are they experienced in the type of construction you are contracting for?
- Do they spend much time at their work sites? Are they accessible for discussion?
- How open are they to suggestion or request for change?
- Did they each supply several references for comparable projects they've completed?
- How do the prices compare? What's their mark-up for the job?
- Are their companies solvent? Do they keep good records?
- What was your first impression when you met them? Did it change during conversation?
- Did they talk down to you or treat you with the respect deserving of a potential employer?
- Are their companies large or small? Can they give your project their personal attention?
- Did you visit their existing job site? What was the attitude of the workers?
- What insurances do they carry? In what amounts?
- Did you review a sample contract? Are they receptive to changes to it?
- What is the general condition of their equipment? Have they had labor problems?
- Which subcontractors do they use? Do you have a say in whom they use?
- Did they visit your lot? What suggestions did they offer?
- How long will it take them to complete the project?

FIXING A BUDGET

It might seem like a play on words, but I chose the phrase *Fixing a Budget* to title this section as opposed to establishing or drawing up a budget for a very sound reason. If you've proceeded this far into the construction process, you, my friend, should by now be totally committed to it. If you aren't, don't sign anything!

At this point you should be painfully aware of what it's going to cost you to appease your lifelong hunger for a custom-built home. But before you position your pen above the dotted line . . .

```
BUDGET


EXCAVATION ,,,,,,,,,,,,,,,,,,,,,,,,,,,,,,,,,,,,,,,,,,,,,,,,,,,,  $    3,277
SITE UTILITIES ,,,,,,,,,,,,,,,,,,,,,,,,,,,,,,,,,,,,,,,,,,,,,,,,       7,310
PAVING ,,,,,,,,,,,,,,,,,,,,,,,,,,,,,,,,,,,,,,,,,,,,,,,,,,,,,,,,       4,257
LANDSCAPING ,,,,,,,,,,,,,,,,,,,,,,,,,,,,,,,,,,,,,,,,,,,,,,,,,,        1,544
CONCRETE / MASONRY ,,,,,,,,,,,,,,,,,,,,,,,,,,,,,,,,,,,,,,,,,,,       39,486
CARPENTRY ,,,,,,,,,,,,,,,,,,,,,,,,,,,,,,,,,,,,,,,,,,,,,,,,,,,,       24,200
INSULATION ,,,,,,,,,,,,,,,,,,,,,,,,,,,,,,,,,,,,,,,,,,,,,,,,,,,        6,733
ROOFING ,,,,,,,,,,,,,,,,,,,,,,,,,,,,,,,,,,,,,,,,,,,,,,,,,,,,,,        2,839
DOORS & WINDOWS ,,,,,,,,,,,,,,,,,,,,,,,,,,,,,,,,,,,,,,,,,,,,,        14,540
DRYWALL ,,,,,,,,,,,,,,,,,,,,,,,,,,,,,,,,,,,,,,,,,,,,,,,,,,,,,,        7,219
PAINTING & WALLCOVERINGS,,,,,,,,,,,,,,,,,,,,,,,,,,,,,,,,,,,,,         8,106
CARPETING ,,,,,,,,,,,,,,,,,,,,,,,,,,,,,,,,,,,,,,,,,,,,,,,,,,,,        8,427
CABINETS / APPLIANCES ,,,,,,,,,,,,,,,,,,,,,,,,,,,,,,,,,,,,,,,,       11,414
H,V,A,C, ,,,,,,,,,,,,,,,,,,,,,,,,,,,,,,,,,,,,,,,,,,,,,,,,,,,,,        5,600
PLUMBING ,,,,,,,,,,,,,,,,,,,,,,,,,,,,,,,,,,,,,,,,,,,,,,,,,,,,,        6,363
ELECTRICAL ,,,,,,,,,,,,,,,,,,,,,,,,,,,,,,,,,,,,,,,,,,,,,,,,,,,        6,972



                              SubTotal           158,287

                              6 % Builders Overhead     9,497

                              11 %  Builders Profit     17,412

                              TOTAL              185,196
```

Fig. 2-5. Preliminary budget summarizing builder's cost.

Considerations

- What did the bank have to say?
- Is the lot purchase locked in? What is the *total* cost of the land?
- Did you obtain an impact fee schedule from your local authority?
- How much will site preparation be? Does that include the cost of permits and fees? Survey?
- What is the revised square footage? Revised cost per square foot?
- Are you planning to install any out buildings? How much will they add to the total?
- What will the total cost of your bank loan be? Did you figure in processing charges?

- Who will pick up the permit, inspection, and utility service connection fees?
- Did you figure in the cost of the drawings? The cost of copies and their distribution?
- How much will it cost you for transportation to and from the site?
- Did you figure a cost for corresponding with your builder by mail and telephone?
- Is paving to be a separate expense or included in the builders agreement?
- Will you be contracting with independents such as interior designers/decorators?
- Have you purchased insurance to protect against "acts of God"?
- Did you add 10% to your bottom line to cover the unforeseen and unpredictable occurrence?
- Did you agree to allowances and selections with the builder? The schedule for draws?

SIGNING THE CONTRACT

Are you sure you checked everything out? Does the design work for you? Great! Do you feel comfortable with the builder? Wonderful! Can you live within the budgetary constraints? Marvelous! But before you sign the agreement I suggest you read the document thoroughly. Here, you can use a magnifying glass to enlarge the small print. Building contracts don't need to be complicated. After reading your contract, you should know . . .

Considerations

- Who are the parties to the contract? Are all copies signed and witnessed? What is the consideration?
- Are all the rights of the owner and builder spelled out? When will construction begin? Be completed?
- Are the survey, drawings, and specifications referred to or included in the document?
- What insurance is required to be purchased by the builder? The owner?
- Does the agreement address material quality? Recourse for poor workmanship?
- How specific is the summary of the work to be performed? Were change orders covered?
- Which codes will be adhered to? Who is responsible for which taxes and fees?
- What schedules and reports can you expect to receive? How often will the owner and builder meet?

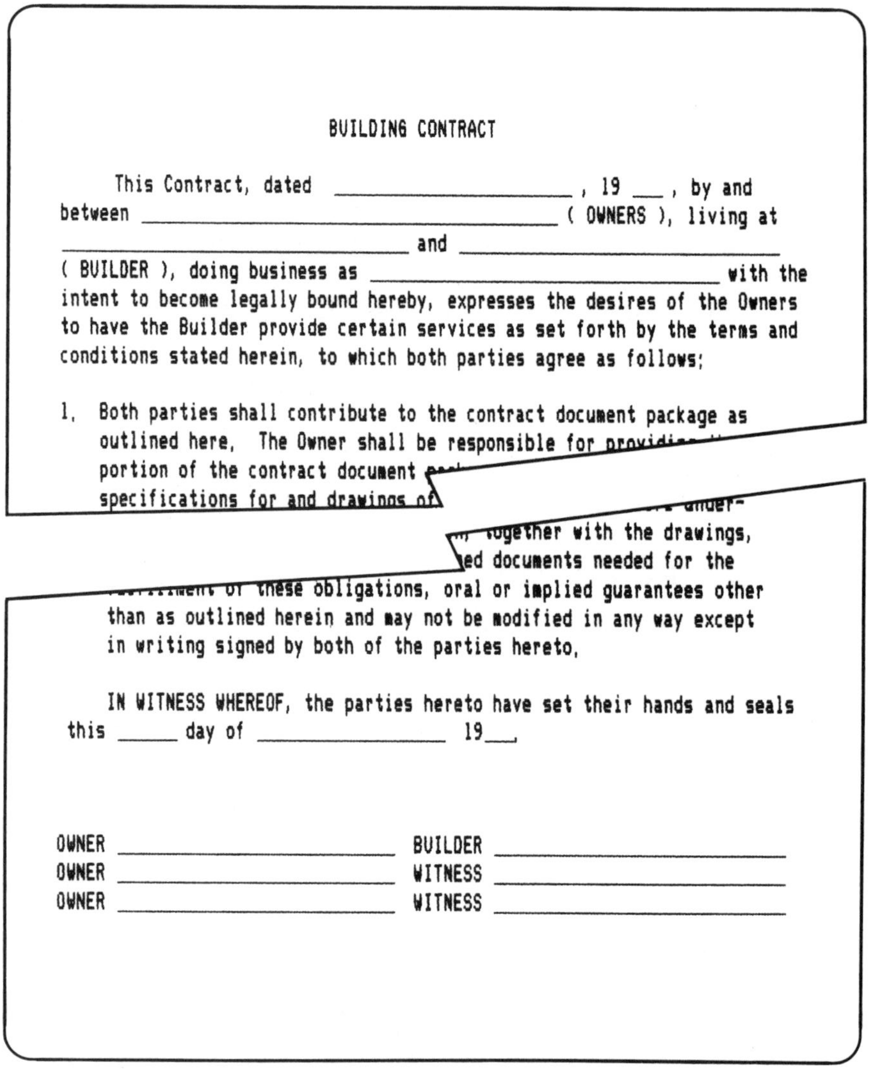

BUILDING CONTRACT

This Contract, dated _____ , 19 ___ , by and
between _____ (OWNERS), living at
_____ and _____
(BUILDER), doing business as _____ with the
intent to become legally bound hereby, expresses the desires of the Owners
to have the Builder provide certain services as set forth by the terms and
conditions stated herein, to which both parties agree as follows;

1. Both parties shall contribute to the contract document package as
    outlined here. The Owner shall be responsible for providing the
    portion of the contract document and
    specifications for and drawings of

                              together with the drawings,
                           ed documents needed for the
    .... of these obligations, oral or implied guarantees other
    than as outlined herein and may not be modified in any way except
    in writing signed by both of the parties hereto.

    IN WITNESS WHEREOF, the parties hereto have set their hands and seals
    this _____ day of _____ 19___.

OWNER _____   BUILDER _____
OWNER _____   WITNESS _____
OWNER _____   WITNESS _____

Fig. 2-6. Front and back of a typical building contract.

- Is there a payment schedule? Are the draws based on reasonable
  completion increments?
- Will the job site be monitored by a full-time supervisor? Who will be
  responsible in his absence?
- How will disputes that arise be resolved? Delays and time extensions
  covered?
- Are you allowed to visit the job site? Can you input your wants to
  the subcontractors?

- Are items such as temporary utilities, barriers, and clean-up mentioned in the document?
- What warranties and guarantees are stated? How long will they remain in effect?
- Did you have a lawyer review the legal aspects of the agreement? Is there a proviso for termination?

SELECTING THE HARDWARE

It appears your involvement in the construction game up to this point has exacted a toll on you. You're developing bags under your eyes, and your fingernails have been chewed to the quick. What a mess! Yes, I know you've invested a lot of time . . . and you've got a pile of money riding on . . . and you don't really know that much about . . . and . . . stop it! For you, the hard part is over. Take a break and choose a motif for your new home. It's time for the contractor to do a little sweating now.

Well, how did you make out? You're certain of all your choices? Fantastic! But don't hand the completed list over to the builder just yet . . .

Considerations

- Does everything properly match or contrast? Can you call for changes later? How much later?
- Did you consult with an interior designer about space? Your family members about what will go into the space?
- What assistance did the builder give you? Can he show you examples in an existing house?
- How involved were you in planning the landscape? Did you choose the bushes and trees? Their location?
- What exterior finish have you chosen for the structure? Will your choice of roof materials clash with the siding?
- Will the exterior doors and hardware be a focal point? Should you have chosen wood instead of metal?
- Are you going to have the appliances built in or will they be free standing? What if you want to move them later?
- Will your cabinets be made of wood or wood products? Will they be stained or painted?
- Have you arranged to have all of your utility wires, pipes, and conduits hidden? Will they be accessible for repair?
- Did you locate the sprinkler heads in the ground? Will you have an outside faucet?
- Do the wall and floor coverings match the materials you've chosen for your countertops?

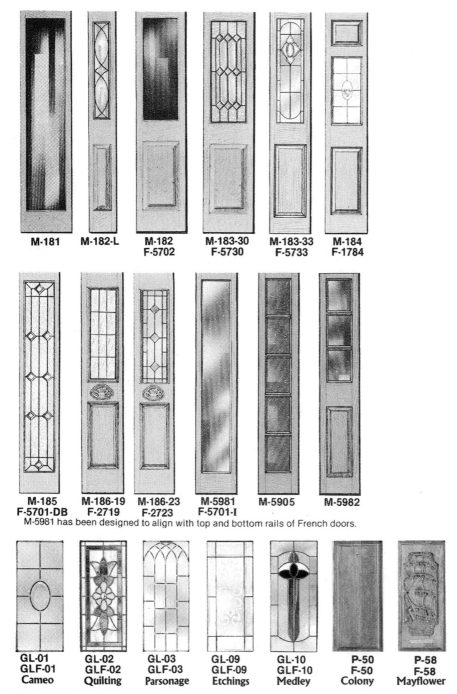

M-181   M-182-L   M-182   M-183-30   M-183-33   M-184
                    F-5702   F-5730   F-5733   F-1784

M-185   M-186-19   M-186-23   M-5981   M-5905   M-5982
F-5701-DB F-2719   F-2723   F-5701-I

M-5981 has been designed to align with top and bottom rails of French doors.

GL-01   GL-02   GL-03   GL-09   GL-10   P-50   P-58   P-59
GLF-01   GLF-02   GLF-03   GLF-09   GLF-10   F-50   F-58   F-59
Cameo   Quilting   Parsonage   Etchings   Medley   Colony   Mayflower Heritage

Fig. 2-7. Entry door sidelight panels & inserts. COURTESY OF MORGAN PRODUCTS, LTD.

- What kinds of ceilings have you specified? Can they accommodate a chandelier or fan?
- Are you having a fireplace installed? Will it be easily accessible for cleaning? Will it have a mantel?
- Did you specify the number and location of additional valves and electrical receptacles?
- Where will the television and telephone lines terminate?

Fig. 2-8. Single story masonry structure with hip rafters set in place.

MONITORING THE CONSTRUCTION

So, how are you and what's-his-name getting along? Good. I think you made the right choice contracting with him. He might be a tad more expensive than the other two, but he's got a fairly lengthy string of satisfied homeowners vouching for him. His operation is still small enough that he can afford you the individual attention you've been looking for. But don't get too comfortable just yet . . .

Considerations

- Have you filed away copies of the survey? The plans? The builder's license? The contract? Test results? Building permits? Performance bonds? Insurance policies? Tax receipts?
- Did you create a working file for construction correspondence? Project meeting minutes? Copies of work schedules? Paid receipts for materials? Change orders?

- What time do the work crews arrive on the job site? When do they leave? How often do you visit the job site?
- Are you kept abreast of changes in the schedule? Are payments being made on time?
- Have there been any labor problems at the site? How were they resolved?
- Do you receive daily progress reports? Copies of inspectors' findings?
- Are you notified promptly concerning materials substitutions? Are monetary adjustments made?
- Do the materials stored at the site appear to be of the proper quality? Quantity?
- Have you reviewed the subcontractors qualifications? History of performance?
- Has the ground been contoured to promote proper drainage of surface water? Has it been compacted in areas where concrete is to be poured?
- Did the builder install a vapor barrier on the exterior of the foundation? Has the soil been treated for pest control?
- Was the proper thickness of insulation installed? Are the drain lines sloped?
- Was the proper thickness of concrete used? Was it reinforced?
- Is the job site kept clear of debris? Is the builder hauling the garbage away or burying it?

Fig. 2-9. Questionable location of electrical receptacle under window sill.

INSPECTING THE PRODUCT

What a fine looking house! May I come in? Thank you. How's that? I'll be glad to tour it with you. After all, you paid a pretty penny for all of this, and I want to make sure you got a good bang for your buck. So, without taking the builder to the bank . . .

Considerations

- Did you compile a punch list of all discrepancies found? Did you review it with the builder?
- Are all the mechanicals in good working order? Were you given a list of telephone numbers to call for resolving problems?
- Was the structure left broom clean? Has all refuse and debris been hauled away?
- Are all the vents clear? From the dryer? The bathrooms? The kitchen's vent hood? The chimney?
- Have ground fault receptacles been installed in all wet areas? Is the electric load properly balanced and grounded?
- Do the appliances work? Door chimes? Burglar alarm? Intercom?
- Is there any evidence of unfinished work? Missing parts? Separated joints?
- Are the floors level? Do they creak? Was the proper covering installed?
- Do the windows and doors swing freely? In the right direction? Are they properly caulked?
- Is anything dented? Torn? Stained? Leaking? Broken? Cracked? Gouged? Buckled? Out of square? Out of plumb? Chipped? Corroded? Burned? Scratched? Collapsed? Mildewed? Out of place? Rough? Unstable?

3

The Principals
and Their Concerns

NOW THAT YOU HAVE SOME IDEA OF THE WORK LOAD YOU'RE GETTING YOUR-
self in for, let me introduce you to the people you'll be involved with in
your attempt to accomplish it. Properly coordinated, the expertise
expended by these individuals on your project will culminate in more
than just a well-constructed house. As a group, their combined efforts
are capable of producing for you a fine home you'll cherish long after
you've progressed into another life phase and sold it to others. Although
their activities often overlap, they work within specific confines of the
project.

ARCHITECT

Architects are book-trained professionals who are licensed by state
governments via examination to practice the art of building design. By
way of education and experience, they often find their niche in specialty
areas such as commercial high-rise structures, bridge construction, or
naval architecture. In the residential building field, their role is not limited to supplying the drawings and specifications for construction projects. They alone interpret those fruits of their labor and approve any
changes made thereto—within the guidelines of the contract of course.
Other of their responsibilities might include validation of contractor
invoices for work performed, verifying material quality, and counseling
with the owner on the appropriateness of proposed changes.

ATTORNEY

Attorneys seem to go to school forever and, like architects, are state licensed. They apply their art to every conceivable aspect of the human condition. As legal advisors to the owners having a house built, they might be called upon to intercede in complicated negotiations; interpret legal contracts, binders, and insurance policies; ascertain your rights when disputes occur; and represent you during litigation should the need arise.

BANKER

Years ago my cousin, Giovanni, and I were perusing the classifieds when I ran across an ad for a *loan arranger*. Though I wasn't interested in pursuing the position, the title had a curious ring to it. So I asked my cousin if he knew what a loan arranger was, to which he replied, "Shu, he'sa Tonto's afren." A rose by any other name . . . ?

The educations of personnel working in financial institutions are as diverse as the services they provide. Generally speaking, the bank itself, not its employees, must be licensed. Nevertheless, certain individuals could be required by corporate policy to be bonded.

The services they normally provide home builders are the issuance of a construction loan, which reverts to a permanent mortgage when the project is finished; fabrication of a disbursement schedule for pay out as work progresses; frequent inspection visits to the job site to ensure proper compliance with all agreements; and acquisition of the proper insurances.

BUILDER

Out of the total flock that makes up mankind, the builder is a rare bird. He could have studied in college, received his training through the school of hard knocks, or combined the two. But, one thing is certain; his skills must be many and continually honed to keep up with the ever changing construction industry. Depending on where he is doing business, the laws regulating his efforts can be either stringent or lax, and licensure can be difficult, and sometimes, impossible.

Though some builders are large enough to maintain their own crews to perform all the work for which they've been contracted, most avail themselves of the assistance provided by individual subcontractors. Typically, builders plan and execute all site preparation work, provide schedules for work completion, order construction materials, coordinate the activities of all construction personnel, attend project meetings, write reports detailing job progress, explain delays, and negotiate change orders with the owner.

INSPECTOR

Construction inspections are made for a multitude of reasons, and the number of inspectors visiting a site will vary from project to project—depending on local ordinances, contractual obligations, and the degree of financial risk posed by the venture to its principals. Inspections are made by utility companies, to ensure that no harm will come to their systems when they are connected; municipal authorities, to ascertain that the structure conforms to applicable building codes; the architect, to check for compliance with his drawings and specifications; the project superintendent, to make certain schedules are met; bank officials, to protect their investment interests; and the owner, to make sure he gets what he pays for.

SUBCONTRACTORS

Subcontractors are specialty work groups generally limited to one trade. They come replete with the correct number of mechanics needed to accomplish the task at hand, one of whom is delegated the responsibility of job foreperson. These crewmen are usually highly skilled technicians who received much of their training on the job, through an apprenticeship program or a vocational school. Naturally, as individuals, they have varying temperaments but are generally viewed as no-nonsense, strictly business kinds of people due to the nature of the contractual agreements they often work under. Time is money! An attempt to list every conceivable trade, occupation, or specialty that you might run into on a home building project would prove futile here. Rather than parade that army by you, what do you say to reviewing the more commonly known workmen? Fine. Here's who they are and some of what they do.

Carpenter. Rough and finish carpentry, framing of walls, construction of concrete forms, sheathing, wood decking, cabinet making, roof construction, installation of wood floors, boxing-in built-in fixtures and appliances, stairwork and railings, paneling, molding and trim installation, and window and door frame and door installation.

Concrete Mason. Constructs footings and foundation; pours walls, floors, stairs, walkways, and drives; waterproofs concrete structures; lays bricks and installs stones in fireplaces, exterior walls, and outbuildings; grouts seams; and installs tile, brick, or stone floors, drives, walkways, and chimney.

Electrician. Installs service entrance panel; wires entire house; installs interior and exterior light fixtures, electrical receptacles, and switches;

connects built-in electrical appliances; runs cable for telephone and television; and installs special circuitry for burglar alarms.

Excavator. Clears, roughs, and finishes grading of land; removes stumps and large rocks; reconfigures land contours for appearance and drainage; and spreads topsoil.

HVAC Mechanic. Installs furnaces, and air conditioners; and supplies and returns air ductwork, grillwork, and insulation.

Plasterer. Installs dry wall sheeting; plasters walls; decorates ceiling work; stuccos exterior surfaces; grouts ceramic tile work; and caulks window and door frames.

Plumber. Connects boilers and hot water heaters; runs hot and cold water supply lines; installs sewage piping and vents; installs lavatories, commodes, bathtubs, and laundry hook-ups.

Roofer/Sider. Lays felt papers and shingles, flashing around openings, aluminum, steel, or vinyl siding, soffit and facia, gutters and downspouts, and gravel stops.

Specialty Groups. Install roof hatches, garbage disposals, swimming pools, skylights, terrariums, jacuzzi tubs, roof ventilation fans, fences, wallpaper, incinerators, gazebos, decorative bridges, barbecue pits, terrazo flooring, greenhouses, storage sheds, hardwood floors, sprinkler systems, perimeter lighting, built-in cabinetry, safes, book cases, lofts, wine cellars, humidifiers/de-humidifiers, wet bars, projection booths, recessed ceilings, sound proof rooms, recreation rooms, gymnasiums, sport and game courts, sound systems, aquariums, studios, classrooms, office space, automatic doors, aviary, darkroom, invalids room, handicap accoutrements, cogeneration appliances, geothermal heating systems, shutters, florida rooms, superinsulation, solar heating, drive and walkway deicers, awnings, air locks, fire suppression systems, decorative railing, work stations, carports, firewood bins, antennas, indirect lighting, lightning arrestors, computerization, wells, septic tanks, and more; control pests; landscape; and decorate the interior.

4

Chasing Paper Down the Communications Trail

BEFORE EMBARKING ON ANY JOURNEY IT'S ALWAYS WISE TO COMPILE AN ITIN-erary. This will be yours for traversing the paper trail ahead. Unlike other sections of this work where topics are addressed alphabetically, the issues you'll peruse here will be covered more or less as you'd be confronted by them in an actual project situation. Bear in mind though, as in real life, points A and B are seldom connected by a straight line. Your vehicle is a four-drawer filing cabinet. Here's a map to help you find your way. Drive carefully and enjoy your trip!

PRELIMINARY PAPERWORK

You can't begin to *think* house until the top drawer of your filing cabinet is crammed with information on all aspects of the land parcel on which it will set. At a minimum, the top drawer should contain:

- photographs of the site taken from several vantage points accompanied by a topographic map of the surrounding area
- a measured sketch of the lot showing the dimensions and proposed location of the dwelling and outbuildings
- a survey and survey narrative showing and describing the location of underground utilities, existing rights of way, and easements
- documented proof that a title search was performed showing the land is owned "free and clear" and all liens and encumbrances against it have been settled

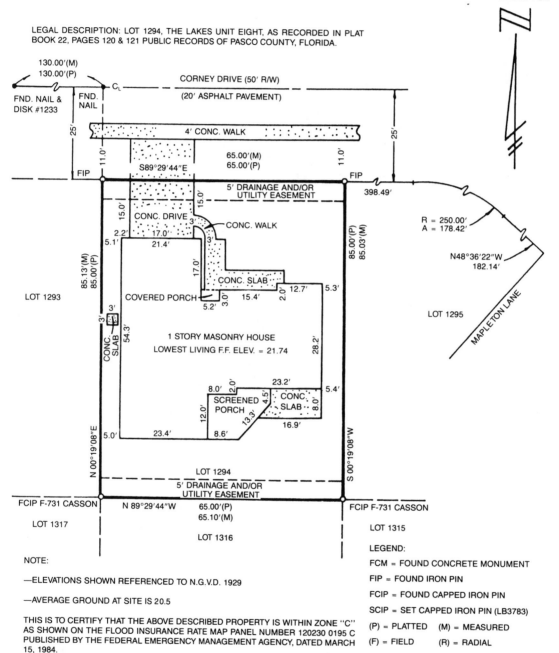

SCALE 1" = 20'

SEC. 23 TWP. 25 S. RNG. 16 E.
BEARINGS BASED UPON RECORD PLAT

LEGAL DESCRIPTION: LOT 1294, THE LAKES UNIT EIGHT, AS RECORDED IN PLAT BOOK 22, PAGES 120 & 121 PUBLIC RECORDS OF PASCO COUNTY, FLORIDA.

130.00'(M)
130.00'(P)

CORNEY DRIVE (50' R/W)

(20' ASPHALT PAVEMENT)

FND. NAIL & DISK #1233
FND. NAIL

4' CONC. WALK

65.00'(M)
65.00'(P)

S89°29'44"E

FIP

FIP

398.49'

5' DRAINAGE AND/OR UTILITY EASEMENT

CONC. DRIVE

CONC. WALK

R = 250.00'
A = 178.42'

N48°36'22"W
182.14'

CONC. SLAB

COVERED PORCH

LOT 1293

CONC. SLAB

1 STORY MASONRY HOUSE
LOWEST LIVING F.F. ELEV. = 21.74

LOT 1295

MAPLETON LANE

SCREENED PORCH

CONC. SLAB

LOT 1294

5' DRAINAGE AND/OR UTILITY EASEMENT

FCIP F-731 CASSON

N 89°29'44"W   65.00'(P)
65.10'(M)

FCIP F-731 CASSON

LOT 1317

LOT 1315

LOT 1316

NOTE:

—ELEVATIONS SHOWN REFERENCED TO N.G.V.D. 1929

—AVERAGE GROUND AT SITE IS 20.5

THIS IS TO CERTIFY THAT THE ABOVE DESCRIBED PROPERTY IS WITHIN ZONE "C" AS SHOWN ON THE FLOOD INSURANCE RATE MAP PANEL NUMBER 120230 0195 C PUBLISHED BY THE FEDERAL EMERGENCY MANAGEMENT AGENCY, DATED MARCH 15, 1984.

LEGEND:

FCM = FOUND CONCRETE MONUMENT
FIP = FOUND IRON PIN
FCIP = FOUND CAPPED IRON PIN
SCIP = SET CAPPED IRON PIN (LB3783)
(P) = PLATTED   (M) = MEASURED
(F) = FIELD   (R) = RADIAL

Fig. 4-1. Certificate of survey.

- results of subsurface investigations describing soil composition/compaction and unusual site conditions such as rock ledges or underground springs
- a sketch of the property showing which trees and bushes are to be saved, the proposed ways of travel, utility tap-ins, disturbed topsoil storage area, and the construction trash pit, if any
- applications for bank loans, utility connections, and curb cuts
- a list of telephone numbers for everyone involved in the project

THE BIDDERS BIN

It's amazing how you compiled all that data on such short notice. You're a fine organizer. At this juncture, you might or might not have drawings and specifications to work from. If you do, file away a clean set in the cabinet. If you don't, it's time to decide what this dream house of yours is going to look like. Whether an architect or a builder supplies your blueprints, it's crucial that you scrutinize him well before you hire him. For obvious reasons, when you submit a request for proposal (RFP) to a company or individual, it makes good sense to get more than one bid. Whenever practical, don't do business unless you have three bids to work from. Make certain that all three were arrived at using the same criteria. This information should be available in the next drawer:

- your written request for quotation spelling out exactly what you want built, with or without an accompanying set of drawings and specifications
- a company brochure from each bidder giving a history of their organization, number of years in business, photo representation of the type of construction they do, and a listing of services they provide
- at least three business references from persons for which work, comparable in magnitude and price, was performed by each bidder
- letters of support from material suppliers stating the number of years they've been doing business with each builder, in what volume, and how promptly the bills were paid
- insurance and bond binders specifying the coverage called for in the RFP or an agent's affirmation that policies and bonds would be issued if the builder applied for them
- copies of company policies covering drinking on the job, theft, and recourse for poor workmanship
- a list of subcontractors used, their job descriptions, and tool inventory
- bids from at least three builders with remarks and opinions covering any gray areas they perceived in the RFP
- each bid containing a detailed cost breakdown of every proposed activity and trade, as well as a proposed budget

CERTIFICATE OF INSURANCE

ISSUE DATE (MM/DD/YY)
10-30-85

PRODUCER

THIS CERTIFICATE IS ISSUED AS A MATTER OF INFORMATION ONLY AND CONFERS NO RIGHTS UPON THE CERTIFICATE HOLDER. THIS CERTIFICATE DOES NOT AMEND, EXTEND OR ALTER THE COVERAGE AFFORDED BY THE POLICIES BELOW.

COMPANIES AFFORDING COVERAGE

COMPANY LETTER	A	Insurance Company
COMPANY LETTER	B	
COMPANY LETTER	C	
COMPANY LETTER	D	
COMPANY LETTER	E	

INSURED

THIS IS TO CERTIFY THAT POLICIES OF INSURANCE LISTED BELOW HAVE BEEN ISSUED TO THE INSURED NAMED ABOVE FOR THE POLICY PERIOD INDICATED. NOTWITHSTANDING ANY REQUIREMENT, TERM OR CONDITION OF ANY CONTRACT OR OTHER DOCUMENT WITH RESPECT TO WHICH THIS CERTIFICATE MAY BE ISSUED OR MAY PERTAIN, THE INSURANCE AFFORDED BY THE POLICIES DESCRIBED HEREIN IS SUBJECT TO ALL THE TERMS, EXCLUSIONS, AND CONDITIONS OF SUCH POLICIES.

CO LTR	TYPE OF INSURANCE	POLICY NUMBER	POLICY EFFECTIVE DATE (MM/DD/YY)	POLICY EXPIRATION DATE (MM/DD/YY)	LIABILITY LIMITS IN THOUSANDS		
						EACH OCCURRENCE	AGGREGATE
	GENERAL LIABILITY						
A	X COMPREHENSIVE FORM		6-17-85	6-17-86	BODILY INJURY	$	$
	PREMISES/OPERATIONS						
	UNDERGROUND EXPLOSION & COLLAPSE HAZARD				PROPERTY DAMAGE	$	$
	PRODUCTS/COMPLETED OPERATIONS						
	CONTRACTUAL				BI & PD COMBINED	$1,000,	$
	INDEPENDENT CONTRACTORS						
	BROAD FORM PROPERTY DAMAGE						
	PERSONAL INJURY				PERSONAL INJURY		$
	AUTOMOBILE LIABILITY						
	ANY AUTO				BODILY INJURY (PER PERSON)	$	
	ALL OWNED AUTOS (PRIV. PASS.)				BODILY INJURY (PER ACCIDENT)	$	
	ALL OWNED AUTOS (OTHER THAN PRIV. PASS.)						
	HIRED AUTOS				PROPERTY DAMAGE	$	
	NON-OWNED AUTOS						
	GARAGE LIABILITY				BI & PD COMBINED	$	
	EXCESS LIABILITY						
	UMBRELLA FORM				BI & PD COMBINED	$	$
	OTHER THAN UMBRELLA FORM						
	WORKERS' COMPENSATION AND EMPLOYERS' LIABILITY				STATUTORY		
					$	(EACH ACCIDENT)	
					$	(DISEASE-POLICY LIMIT)	
					$	(DISEASE-EACH EMPLOYEE)	
	OTHER						

DESCRIPTION OF OPERATIONS/LOCATIONS/VEHICLES/SPECIAL ITEMS

Construction

Fig. 4-2. Certificate of insurance.

Borough of Grove City

1328 WEST MAIN STREET
GROVE CITY, PENNSYLVANIA 16127
TELEPHONE (412) 458-7060

PLUMBER'S LICENSE BOND

KNOW ALL MEN BY THESE PRESENTS, That _____
_____ and _____ .
Surety, are held and firmly bound unto the BOROUGH OF GROVE CITY,
Mercer County, Pennsylvania, in the sum of Two Thousand (2,000.00)
Dollars lawful money of the United States of America, for the payment
of which, well and truly to be made to said BOROUGH OF GROVE CITY or
its certain attorney, we do bind ourselves, our heirs, administrators,
executors, successors and assigns.

In Witness whereof, we have hereunto set our hands and seals

this _____ day of _____ , 19___ .

WHEREAS, the said _____

has been granted a permit by the said BOROUGH OF GROVE CITY for a

period of one year, expiring _____ for plumbing

work in the BOROUGH OF GROVE CITY.

NOW, THEREFORE, THE CONDITION OF THIS OBLIGATION IS SUCH,

That if the said _____

its heirs, executors, successors, or assigns, shall engage in plumbing

work within the Borough of Grove City in accordance with the provisions

of Ordinance No. 835, enacted the 16th day of November, 1964, this

obligation to be void otherwise to remain in full force and effect.

WITNESS:

_____   _____ (SEAL)

WITNESS:

_____   _____ (SEAL)

Fig. 4-3. Plumber's license bond. COURTESY OF THE BOROUGH OF GROVE CITY, GROVE CITY, PA.

CONSTRUCTION CORRESPONDENCE

If you've ventured this far into the text I can only surmise that you've reviewed the requested bids and decided on a contractor. You notice I said I surmised, not *assumed* you chose a builder. It might seem like a play on words to you, but nothing should ever be *assumed* in the construction game.

If you aren't already aware of the universal principle supporting this contention, let me spell it out for you. When you consider the combinations of possible problems that can result from inputting the variables associated with any given project, there's a 100 percent chance that when you *assume* the outcome, you'll end up making an *ass* out of *u* and *me*. So don't take for granted that you have everything on file. Open the third drawer, and make certain you have:

- the master plan showing what is to be done and by what date it's to be accomplished
- witnessed copies of all contracts and subcontractor agreements signed and dated by all applicable parties
- copies of workmen's compensation, liability, and "act of God" insurance policies and bonds
- approved application forms for utility connections and copies of granted permits
- the drawings, specifications, construction schedule, and worker instructions
- approved construction loan, budget, schedule of draws, and associated sign-off sheets
- the bank's Notice of Commencement
- a list of agreed-upon selections, approved purchase orders, invoices, and bills of lading
- copies of project meeting minutes and daily progress reports signed by the builder or site supervisor

THE FINALIZING FILE

I spent a good half-hour trying to track down a source for who said, "It's not over 'till it's over," and finally confirmed that it was Yogi Berra who first said it. But no matter, I'm here to tell you that, in the building field, it's never totally over. First, there's the guarantee to consider; then a time period before the warranties, both written and implied expire; there are statutes of limitations for recovery from damages; not to mention precedent-setting litigation initiated by industrious attorneys in settling consumer claims. Don't overlook the conscience and profes-

ER—BWQ—291: Rev. 4-84
(Formerly ER—BCE—129)

*SEE REVERSE SIDE FOR IMPORTANT INFORMATION

PERMIT
for
INSTALLATION OF SEWAGE DISPOSAL SYSTEM

Pursuant to Application for Sewage Disposal System number _____
a permit is hereby issued to:

NAME OF APPLICANT

ADDRESS OF APPLICANT   TELEPHONE NUMBER

PROPERTY ADDRESS OF SITE FOR SEWAGE DISPOSAL SYSTEM

This Permit issued under the provisions of the "Pennsylvania Sewage Facilities Act", the Act of January 24, 1966 (P.L. 1535), as amended is subject to the following conditions:

1. Except as otherwise provided by the Act or regulations of the Pennsylvania Department of Environmental Resources, no part of the installation shall be covered until inspected by the approving body and approval to cover is granted in writing below.

2. This Permit may be revoked for the reasons set forth in Section 7(b)(6) of the Act.

3. If construction or installation of an individual sewage system or community sewage system and of any building or structure for which such system is to be installed has not commenced within two years after the issuance of a permit for such system, the said permit shall expire, and a new permit shall be obtained prior to the commencement of said construction or installation.

ADDITIONAL CONDITIONS:

KEEP THIS PERMIT FOR FUTURE REFERENCE

Approval to Cover   Date of Issuance of Permit _____

_____   _____
Signature of Enforcement Officer   Approving Body

_____   _____
Date   Signature of Enforcement Officer

The basis for the issuance of this Permit is the information supplied in the Application for Sewage Disposal System and other pertinent data concerning soil absorption tests, topography, lot size, and sub-soil groundwater table elevations. The permit only indicates that the issuing authority is satisfied that the installation of the Sewage Disposal System is in accordance with the Rules, Regulations and Standards adopted by the Pennsylvania Department of Environmental Resources under the provisions of the Pennsylvania Sewage Facilities Act, the Act of January 24, 1966 (P.L. 1535), as amended. The issuance of a Permit shall not preclude the enforcement of other health laws, ordinances or regulations in the case of malfunctioning of the system.

TO BE POSTED AT THE BUILDING SITE

FORM PROVIDED BY THE PENNSYLVANIA DEPARTMENT OF ENVIRONMENTAL RESOURCES

Fig. 4-4. Sewage disposal system installation permit.

sionalism of the builder himself in "making it right." But there comes a point in the construction process where building ceases, and any further attention paid to a project is considered new work, which costs money! Effectively, it is reached concomitantly with the clearing of your last check in the builder's bank account. Before you release the final funds, check drawer number four for:

- the signed guarantee
- all the warranties and the telephone numbers of the persons you are to contact to honor them
- a complete list of approved material substitutions and approved change orders
- correspondence from the builder agreeing to additional work
- pictures of the project through all phases of construction
- a signed punchlist of discrepancies, which the builder has agreed to redo, found during the owner/builder joint inspection.

ANALYZING THE CONTRACT

Even though we might not fully understand them, we've all had to live with contracts at one time or another in our lives. Contracts are entered into every time a person marries, joins a group, or buys a car. The fact is, that almost anything we do involves a contract; whether written or implied.

So, what's a *contract*? I define it as a legal obligation between people whereby one party is required to deliver a product or service to another in return for something agreed upon. To my children, that equates to receiving an allowance for keeping their rooms tidy. Though this same simple principle applies to all agreements, not surprisingly, a construction contract is much more complicated than that. The contract itself is actually a package of documents of which the agreement is only one part. The remainder of the contract documents include conditions that support the agreement, drawings, specifications, and other miscellaneous addenda that supplement or amend the agreement after its execution. Generally a construction contract contains:

- the name of all concerned parties
- a description of the project
- start-up and completion dates
- the rights of the owner
- the duties of the builder
- reference to drawings/specifications
- payment schedules
- insurance/bond requirements
- responsibility for taxes/fees
- guarantee/warranty information
- procedures for claims/disputes

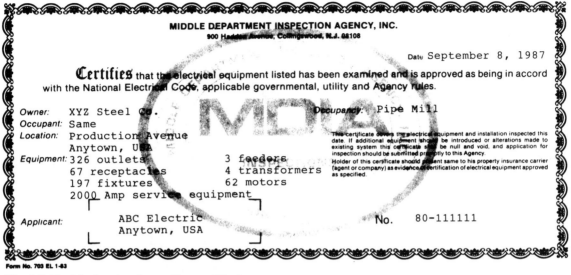

MIDDLE DEPARTMENT INSPECTION AGENCY, INC.
900 Haddon Avenue, Collingwood, N.J. 08108

Date September 8, 1987

Certifies that the electrical equipment listed has been examined and is approved as being in accord with the National Electrical Code, applicable governmental, utility and Agency rules.

Owner: XYZ Steel Co.   Occupancy: Pipe Mill
Occupant: Same
Location: Production Avenue
            Anytown, USA
Equipment: 326 outlets   3 feeders
            67 receptacles   4 transformers
            197 fixtures   62 motors
            2000 Amp service equipment

This certificate covers the electrical equipment and installation inspected this date. If additional equipment should be introduced or alterations made to existing system this certificate shall be null and void, and application for inspection should be submitted promptly to this Agency.
Holder of this certificate should present same to his property insurance carrier (agent or company) as evidence of certification of electrical equipment approved as specified.

Applicant: ABC Electric   No.   80-111111
                Anytown, USA

Form No. 703 EL 1-83

Fig. 4-5. Electrical system inspection certificate.

Customarily, these sections are part and parcel of the agreement:

General Provisions. The definitions of the project implements, an explanation of the overall intent, and a delineation of document ownership.

Owner. The owner's rights and responsibilities.

Builder. The builder's rights and responsibilities.

Contract Administration. The duties of the person empowered to administer the contract, establishes time limits for claims, and dictates how disputes are to be resolved.

Subcontractors. Group to whom the work will be subcontracted; states how it will be awarded, and the relationships between subcontractors, and other parties to the agreement.

Other Contractors. The owner's option to perform a portion of the work or to enter into a separate agreement for performance of a portion of the work by others.

Work Changes. Reasons for and procedures to be used when making minor and major changes to the agreed-upon construction directives.

Time. Commencement date for the project; determines reasonableness of progress over time, sets completion date, and addresses delays and extensions involving time.

Payment Schedule. Cost of the project; ascertains the value of partially completed work, sets increments for payment, and states the penalties for nonpayment and defective workmanship.

Fig. 4-6. Municipal building permit. COURTESY OF THE BOROUGH OF GROVE CITY, GROVE CITY, PA.

Safety. Reasonable standards of safety for the protection of all persons and property connected with the performance of the contract; and establishes the builder's discretionary authority to act in emergency situations.

Insurance/Bonds. Insurance and the amounts to be in force during the contract period to eliminate the financial risks associated with liability, physical injury, death, property damage, and nonperformance of work.

Work Correction. Immediate correction of work determined by the contract administrator to be defective; spells out the time limits for the request and accomplishment of the work.

Miscellany. A catch-all for any item or topic not otherwise covered in another section of the agreement covering such things as meeting schedules, codes and laws, assignments of the agreement, interest payments, . . . etc.

Contract Termination. Termination of the agreement by any or all parties; determines the distribution of assets as the result of termination.

If you don't recall one other thing from all of my ramblings, remember this; the agreement is *the* single most important aspect of the whole construction project. It is the sun in the project universe. Everything else revolves around its construction, language, and execution. By all means, keep a copy of the contract in the file cabinet to reference from time to time, but keep the original tucked away in a fire protected, secure area in your home or in a safe deposit box at a bank.

5

Establishing the
Owner's Master Plan

OKAY, FOLKS. WE'VE TALKED THIS THING TO DEATH. YOU HAVE TO DECIDE IF you're going to ponder or wander. Say what? Sure, that's just a polite way of stating "it's time to sit or get off the pot." Good choice! Let's put together a schedule listing our expectations, and see how it hangs with the rest of the group. Don't worry, you can always modify it later to accommodate the others as needed.

PROJECT PHASING

No two projects have ever been approached in exactly the same way. There are just too many variables to consider in their implementation. Some of the principles might be new to the game, or the crew might be used to working on large or small projects. Prices, quality, and availability of materials can cause postponement or cancellation of all or part of the project. The same holds true for the trades and crafts to be used. Problems with the construction loan can arise at the bank, or the builder might not be able to accommodate the proposed schedule. The list of possibilities is endless. But even though no template exists that enables the rubber stamping of all construction projects, there is a common pattern evident in all of them.

All work, if it is to be properly accomplished, must evolve through the metamorphic process called *phasing*. To my mind, there are five stages or phases associated with any contracted job, regardless of its type or size.

They are visualization, agreement, preparation, actualization, and acceptance—in that order. These five phases can be compared to the old-fashioned strings of Christmas lights that used to drive us up a tree when they'd go out. I know! I know! Where's your holiday spirit? Just as those lights were wired in series, so are these phases dependent on a sequence to work. If any of them are missing, the project will fail.

Please understand that the master plan we'll be putting together will merely guide your mind's eye in maintaining the project in its proper perspective. By no means is it intended to serve as a comprehensive schedule of every project activity. You'll find that each principle involved in the operation will have a particular time frame to which you'll more than likely conform, by way of compromise, early on in the proceedings. Generally speaking, here's how the process works.

Visualization (Weeks 1 through 12)

Nothing created by man can be conceived unless it is first perceived in his mind. In other words, nothing man-made can exist unless it's first thought of. That might sound a little heady, but if you give it some time you'll see the truth—if not the wisdom in that statement.

So, starting with the notion that you would rather have a home built around your lifestyle than pay rent to a landlord, let's put your schedule together. We'll list the activities you anticipate will occur during the course of the project, in the order you expect them to happen, and attempt to forecast the time frames for implementation in project weeks.

Activity by Week	[01]	[02]	[03]	[04]	[05]	[06]
Tour interesting areas	———					
Talk to neighbors	———					
Buy a filing cabinet	—					
Develop preliminary budget		———				
Visit a realtor		—				
Retain an attorney				———		
Choose a potential lot				———		
Review survey / narrative				———		
Review title search				———		
Search court dockets				———		
Check zoning restrictions				———		
Contact utility companies				———		
Purchase land					———	

How's that for a quicky projection? It appears from the schedule that you'll be touring the communities of interest to you and querying people in those neighborhoods the first two weeks. In the second week, you'll buy a file cabinet and begin developing a budget to put into it. During the third week . . . pardon me? No, I don't mind at all. You're absolutely right. You can read the schedule as well as I can, so there's no sense in me reading it to you. Here's the remainder of the schedule for the visualization phase. If you have any questions, feel free to ask them.

Activity by Week	[07]	[08]	[09]	[10]	[11]	[12]
Determine house size	___					
R.F.Q. 3 architects	___					
Architects' bids due	_____					
Review architects' bids				_____		
Check architects' references				_____		
Select architect				_____		
Discuss project ramifications				_____		
Decide on material quality				___		
Review preliminary drawings					_____	
Change drawings and specs						_____
Approve revised documents						_____

Agreement (Weeks 13 through 24)

Nothing constructive can be produced if the parties responsible for its production are in a state of discord. As you can see, you'll be spending the next twelve weeks checking references, reviewing agreements, and deciding on the people you'll be working with for the next few months. This is a crucial period in the process. The decisions you make at this juncture will set the tone for the remainder of the project. Here are the schedules. Is there anything you want to add to them?

Activity by Week	[13]	[14]	[15]	[16]	[17]	[18]
R.F.Q. 3 builders	___					
Supply bid packets	___					
Builders' bids due		_____				
Review builders' bids			_____			
Check builders' references			_____			
Select builder			_____			
Contract review by attorney				_____		
Review revised contract					_____	
Get subcontractor list					_____	
Review subs' agreements					_____	
Approve subcontractors						___

Activity by Week	[19]	[20]	[21]	[22]	[23]	[24]
Hire builder	—					
Supply work documents	—					
Sign contract	—					
Meet with all parties	—					
Apply for construction loan	—					
Notice of commencement		———				
Site visit with builder		———				
Discuss project ramifications			———			
Make initial selections				———		

Preparation (Weeks 25 through 30)

If the lowly mallard knows enough to forgo a trip until she's got all her ducks in a row, shouldn't we have the common sense not to journey unprepared into as involved an endeavor as a construction project? Even a young Boy Scout knows to be prepared before taking on a task, however big.

This point in the project is where the planning you've done in the prior two phases begins to pay dividends. It's the beginning of the realization of your dream, the actual, physical preparation for the construction work that's to follow, and concrete evidence that you didn't really lose your mind after all. Your list looks just ducky, why don't we . . . okay, so I apologize already. There's no need to get into a foul mood every time I ruffle your feathers. Here's duck number one.

Activity by Week	[25]	[26]	[27]	[28]	[29]	[30]
Temporary utilities installed	—					
Trees & shrubs boxed	—					
Land cleared / graded	—					
Property boundaries staked	———					
Utility locations flagged	———					
Debris cleared away	———					
Excavation completed		———				
Footings / foundations poured			———			
Conduits stubbed in			———			
Slabs poured			———			
Foundation waterproofed				———		
House framed				———		
Sheathing applied						—

Actualization (Weeks 31 through 42)

Seeing, it's said, is believing. Well believe me during this phase when you see how quickly the house goes up, and your bank balance goes down, you'll acquire a new appreciation for the term *posthaste*. But hopefully you'll have done your homework, and this will be the least bumpy stretch of your trip as you ride your builders' tails to the end of the line.

Regardless of the validity of your makeshift schedule in terms of time, the fact is that all construction projects can be divided into two parts: rough-in and finish work. *Rough-in* is the ugly side of the process where the bulk of the work is actually performed, but the results often mislead the observer into feeling nothing is being accomplished. This is typical of what goes on.

Activity by Week	[31]	[32]	[33]	[34]	[35]	[36]
Exterior veneer applied	―――	―――	―――			
Roof / chimney built	――	――				
Vents & fans installed	――	――				
Floors finished		――	――			
Underlayment installed			――	――		
Electrical roughed-in				――	――	
Mechanicals roughed-in				――	――	
Plumbing roughed-in				――	――	
Insulation installed					―	
Drywall completed					――	――
Gutters / downspouts installed						―

The second half of the process is where it all comes together for the owners. It's a veritable, sensual feast for their eyes, ears, nose, and touch. The owners finally walk into the rooms that they once only envisioned. The silence of the finishing process has a soothing effect compared to the chaotic din not long before endured. The house smells new, and the plushness of the newly laid carpet can be felt underfoot. It was worth waiting for, wasn't it? If everything goes according to plan, this will occur in the second half of the construction process.

Activity by Week	[37]	[38]	[39]	[40]	[41]	[42]
Cabinetry / shelving installed	――	――				
Electrical finished	―					
Mechanicals finished	―					
Plumbing finished	―					
Interior trimmed out		――	――			
Ceramic work completed			―			
Priming / painting completed				――	――	
Wallcoverings finished				――	――	
Floor completed				――	――	
Drives / walkways paved					――	――
Specialty items installed						―

Acceptance (Weeks 43 through 48)

It often happens that the construction process is completed just prior to the holidays or some other larger-than-life event that makes you anxious to move into your new castle. Some think that builders plan it that way. No so. After all, you're the one who decided on the schedule, aren't you? If the holidays are approaching near the end of the job, chances are the builder is just trying to finish up in time for everyone to enjoy them, especially his employees who would otherwise receive premium wages for their labor. Don't give into the urge, however strong, to move in prematurely. Make certain these items are handled first.

Activity by Week	[43]	[44]	[45]	[46]	[47]	[48]
Interior broom-cleaned	____					
Utilities connected	____					
Land graded	____					
Topsoil replaced	____					
Landscaping completed		_____				
Fencing installed			_____			
Exterior cleaned				_____		
Final inspection made				_____		
Builder reviewed punchlist					_____	
All rework completed					_____	
Project approved						____

6

Selected Construction Tools and Materials

ALTHOUGH I'D BE IMPRESSED IF YOU COULD NAME AND DESCRIBE THE USE OF every item you might run into on a building project, it isn't requisite to your success in its completion. But it stands to reason if you're going to supervise such an endeavor, you should be able to relate to the implements used in carrying it out. A complete lexicon of tools and materials used in the construction trades would fill volumes. This representative sampling should suffice in providing you with the understanding you'll need to survive the ordeal.

ADHESIVES

Adhesives are synthetic glues that hold materials together. They come in liquid and semisolid form and are used where mechanical fastening is undesirable, inappropriate, or in conjunction with fasteners to provide added holding power. Those commonly employed in the building trades include: contact cement for bonding nonporous materials, such as kitchen and bathroom counter tops; mastics for installing flooring, drywall, and paneling; carpenter's glue for attachment of wood surfaces; and a variety of other products too numerous to mention here.

CONDUIT

Generally speaking, a *conduit* is a tube or trough through which pipes, wires, or fluids are passed in order to direct them to a specified point.

Conduits are also used to protect their contents from inadvertent damage caused by intrusions, such as drilling holes or hammering nails into walls. The conduits used to house water, steam, and gas lines, such as those run through concrete slabs, are PVC pipes that are 2 to 4 inches in diameter. The conduits containing electrical wiring include thin-wall EMT (electric metallic tubing), and rigid conduit, which has thicker walls for threading and *greenfield*—a flexible conduit fashioned by spiralling strips of metal into a tubular shape. Pipes through which any fluid flows are also often referred to as conduits.

Fig. 6-1. Assorted sizes of polyvinylchloride (PVC) piping.

COVERINGS

What would the builder do without his coverings. Not only do they make things appealing to the eye, but they cover those multitudes of sins we discussed in the first chapter. Coverings fall into a wide variety of types and applications and are manufactured from a plethora of materials in an infinite array of patterns, colors, and hues. They include veneers for surfacing counters, shelves, doors, and cabinets; floor-coverings consisting of wooden squares, sheet vinyl, vinyl or clay tiles, and carpeting; wallcoverings in the form of vinyl sheet, wallpaper, wood paneling, or tudor and plaster combinations. They can cover a whole wall, the base of a wall as in wainscoting, or a section of a room, accenting the remaining area. There are three factors that effect your choices of coverings: their availability, your imagination, and the depth of your pocketbook.

FASTENERS

If it weren't for fasteners, our whole world would literally fall apart. Appropriately then, they are the mechanical devices man has created to physically hold things together. They come in a myriad of types, configurations, sizes, material compositions, and grade specifications, depending on the jobs for which they are used. Each is designed for an intended purpose. Fasteners include tack strips for installing carpets, corrugated fasteners for joining mitered corners, wood structures and frames, turnbuckles for drawing cables taut, straps for positioning pipes and conduits, nailing plates to hold together truss members, toggle bolts for attachment to hollow walls, staples for fastening roof shingles, rivets, carriage bolts, all thread, wire nuts, and countless other contrivances made especially to help us keep it all together.

Fig. 6-2. PVC pipe cutter. COURTESY OF THE RIDGE TOOL COMPANY, ELYRIA , OH 44036-2023.

HAND TOOLS

Magic mushrooms have no more mesmerizing effect than that of the deft motion of a tool in the hands of a master craftsman. With one swipe, a plasterer can turn gunk into design, and a painter can make metal look like wood. A turn of a plumber's wrench brings water, and the twist of an electrician's pliers can light up your life. I'm sure you're familiar with many of the tools tradesmen carry in their pouches; the hammers that bend nails, the tape measures that contain an extra inch, the screwdrivers that pop the circuit breakers . . . etc. Let me acquaint you with some tools, though common to construction sites, you might not readily recognize.

Broad Knife. A taping knife, similar to a putty knife, but having a wide, flexible metal blade; commonly 12 inches in length; used for finish applications of joint compound to drywall seams.

Chalk Line Reel. A metal or plastic hand-held container in which a coiled string and colored powder is stored. When extracted, it is used to mark long straight lines on flat surfaces. It is also called a *snapline* and sometimes doubles as a plumb bob in a pinch.

Conduit Benders. Devices used to bend thin and heavy wall conduit into specified configurations for routing wiring around obstacles or structures.

Fig. 6-3. Electrical conduit benders. COURTESY OF THE RIDGE TOOL COMPANY, ELYRIA, OH 44036-2023.

Contour Gauge. A metal channel containing numerous plastic or metal pins that, when held against an object, takes on its shape forming a template to transfer the information used to make odd-shaped cuts in materials.

Framing Square. An L-shaped steel rule having a long section (the blade) and a short section (the tongue) that contains common carpentry demarcations used for layout work. It checks the squareness or flatness of surfaces. Other names for the tool are square, builders' square, steel square, rafter square, flat square, and carpenters' square.

Hammers.

1. ripping claw—used in flooring work
2. curved claw—used to pull nails
3. masons—used to position and cut bricks
4. ballpein—used in sheet metal work
5. half-hatchet—used for miscellaneous demolition
6. sledge or maul—used to drive stakes and spikes
7. short-handled sledge—used to cut stone
8. engineer—also known as blacksmith
9. tinners'—used for tacking and metal work

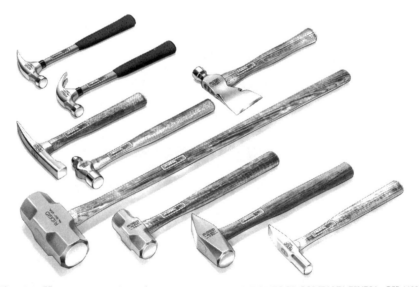

Fig. 6-4. Hammer assortment. COURTESY OF THE RIDGE TOOL COMPANY, ELYRIA, OH 44036-2023.

Levels. Liquid-filled indicators that show whether surfaces are horizontally level or vertically in square. Some common levels are the carpenter's level, also known as a spirit or bubble level; a smaller version, called a *torpedo* or canoe level for use in confined spaces; line levels, used to check the trueness of brick layers lines; and the bull's-eye used to spot check surfaces over a range of 360 degrees.

Plumb Bob. A short, heavy weight tapered to a point and suspended by a cord used to determine the true vertical of structures as compared to its plumb line.

Torch Kit. An assemblage of accessories for delivering and regulating the pressure of bottled acetylene used in cutting and welding metals. Figure 6-5 shows handle and valve assembly, torch tip, hose, regulator, box end wrench, flint spark lighter, and enameled carrying case.

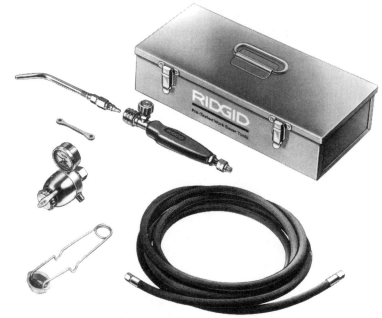

Fig. 6-5. Air-acetylene torch kit. COURTESY OF THE RIDGE TOOL COMPANY, ELYRIA, OH 44036-2023.

HARDWARE

How's that? Well, if you're really that heavy into semantics, and you want to push the argument, I suppose I can concede your point. But just because those things can be purchased at a hardware store, doesn't make them anymore hardware than the materials and power tools we'll be discussing in the next section. Subtle nuances attached to construction terms over many years have caused different people to conjure up diverse meanings for the same words. Would you like a rule-of-thumb to help you weed it all out? Fine. Tools are the devices used by tradesmen to work on materials; materials are the substances used by craftsmen to create an end product; hardware is any component added to the product that makes it complete. Examples are window latches, the brass accessories installed on doors or the handles, and knobs used on cabinetry.

Fig. 6-6. (TRIMMED DOOR)—Your front door is the first impression people have of your house. By giving extra attention to detail, you can create a warm and elegant welcome for your guests. The gleaming solid brass lock trim, kick plate, house numbers, bell button, and letter box plate from Baldwin Hardware Corporation have given this otherwise ordinary entryway prominence.

MATERIALS

As I've just described, materials aren't end products in and of themselves but the stuff from which they are made. Yes, of course a prehung door is a finished product when it leaves the plant, but it can't be used as

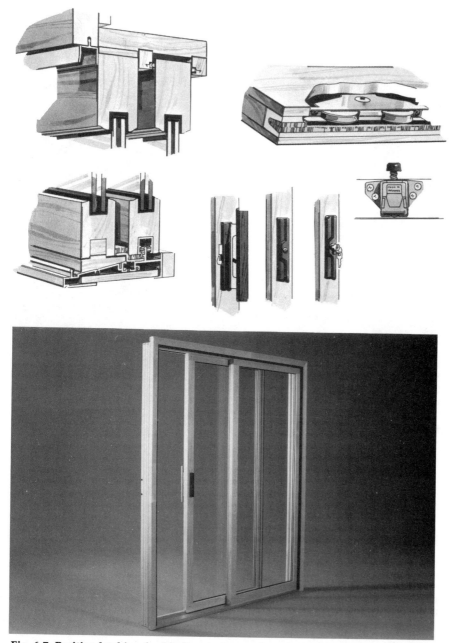

Fig. 6-7. Positive-latching dead bolt superimposed over sliding glass door to which it will be attached. COURTESY OF MORGAN PRODUCTS, LTD.

a door until it's installed. You still don't get it, do you? Anything manufactured can be construed as a product. Until it is in place and functional, it's not an end product. Let's run down this list to help you better comprehend what I'm saying.

Doors. Single or double leaf/flush, paneled, or sash structures made of metal, wood, or wood products that swing or slide. Figure 6-8 shows an exploded view of the parts used to assemble a paneled wood door. The vertical center pieces form the mullion, the horizontal members are rails, and the side pieces are stiles. What's left? Panels, of course.

Fig. 6-8. Exploded view of wooden paneled door. COURTESY OF MORGAN PRODUCTS, LTD.

Insulation. A material that slows down the rate of heat transfer into and out of a structure. Materials commonly used in home building include foil-backed fiberglass blankets, wool batts or foam boards installed between studs, joists, and rafters; rigid sheathing applied to the exterior of foundations; extruded polystyrene pumped into the hollows of foundations; and loose fibrous fill made of cellulose, fiberglass, or vermiculite, which is poured or blown into cavities.

Fig. 6-9. Insulation covered with plastic awaiting drywall installation.

Lumber. Wood comes in two types: hardwood, from trees such as birch, oak, and poplar; and softwood from cedar, spruce, and pine. Hardwoods are graded by descending quality as firsts, seconds, select, and No.s 1, 2, 3A, and 3B common. They are used for finish work such as decorative molding or trimming out wood surfaces. Softwoods are classed as select grades, B or better, C, and D for finish work and common grades; or No. 1—select merchantable, No. 2—construction, No. 3—standard, No. 4—utility, and No. 5—economy.

Once cut, wood is categorized as timber, the smallest dimension of which exceeds 5 inches; dimension lumber, such as 1×2's or 4×4's; and lumber products from waferboard through veneered plywoods. Lumber is often pressure-treated to resist decay, insect, and fungus attack.

PIPES AND FITTINGS

Pipes are the conduits through which fluids flow. They transport potable drinking water, hot water for bathing, and steam and hot water for heat, and natural gas. They are also used to supply water to lawn sprinklers, vent sewer gas from sewage lines, dispose of waste effluent, and act as drain lines for storm water run-off. Pipes are made of metal or plastic and are attached to fixtures with a variety of fittings that are either soldered, glued, or threaded to complete the connection.

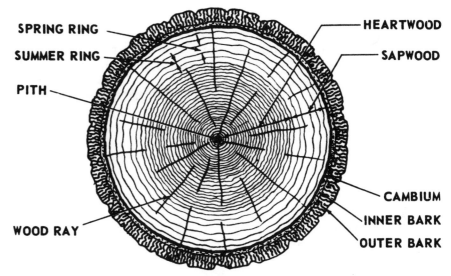

Fig. 6-10. Cross section of a tree. COURTESY OF THE BUREAU OF NAVAL PERSONNEL.

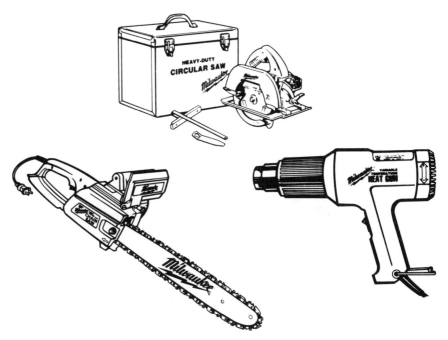

Fig. 6-11. Power tools. COURTESY OF MILWAUKEE ELECTRIC TOOL CORP., BROOKFIELD, WI 53005.

POWER TOOLS

Master craftsmen can produce an endless variety of beautiful and functional items using only handtools, their knowledge of materials, and their abilities to create. Enhance their efforts with power tools, and you'll get the same results or better, sooner. Modern-day economics dictates that, in order to be profitable, more must be produced in less time. By no one is this fact better understood than the blue collar worker who makes a living using tools. These are the tools most frequently utilized on building projects.

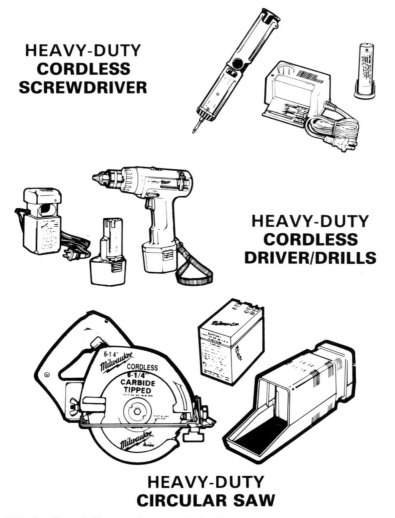

HEAVY-DUTY CORDLESS SCREWDRIVER

HEAVY-DUTY CORDLESS DRIVER/DRILLS

HEAVY-DUTY CIRCULAR SAW

Fig. 6-12. Cordless drill, screwdriver, and circular saw. COURTESY OF MILWAUKEE ELECTRIC TOOL CORP., BROOKFIELD, WI 53005.

Cordless Power Tools. As they become less bulky, weigh less, produce more torque, and come with batteries that hold their charges longer, cordless power tools are used more often in place of the plug-in type. They pose less of a safety hazard than their plug-in cousins, eliminate trips over cords and severe electrical shock, and at the same time, allow mechanics to work in hard to reach places away from their main source of electricity.

Pipe Threader. Why? I don't know, but it seems that when people outside of the trade come into contact with pipe threaders they stand totally

Fig. 6-13. Automatic oiling power drive. COURTESY OF THE RIDGE TOOL COMPANY, ELYRIA, OH 44036-2023.

and completely agog in their presence. Believe me when I tell you there's nothing magical here; it simply makes threads on the ends of pipes.

Router. A router is a device having a high speed shaft to which a variety of bits can be attached to cut grooves and notches into wood, trim the edges of plastic-laminate countertops, or create decorative edging or molding.

Fig. 6-14. Heavy duty router. COURTESY OF MILWAUKEE ELECTRIC TOOL CORP., BROOKFIELD, WI 53005.

Saws and Sanders. You might wonder why I mention these two appliances in the same breath; frankly, it's because materials that are sawed generally have to be sanded afterwards. Whether a saw is stationary or portable, it has a single function—to cut material. Saws aren't the exclusive province of carpenters nor are they confined to the cutting of only wood. Reciprocating saws are used by HVAC mechanics to accommodate duct penetrations through framing members and drywall, electricians and plumbers use holesaws to make circular openings in floors and bulkheads to provide passage for their conduits, and sheet metal and siding mechanics often employ band saws to cut metallic materials. Sanders are used to remove burrs from cut materials, level out high points, and provide a smooth surface. The more common types are the belt sander, having an in-line oscillating motion and the orbital sander, having a rotary motion.

Vacuum Cleaner. Vacuum cleaners, often called shop vacs or wet vacs, are an absolute necessity in construction work. They are driven by heavy-duty electric motors and have large capacity canisters for removing large particulate matter and small pools of water.

WOOD RENDERINGS

The process of working or turning wood at a job site is no longer a cost-effective proposition. These days, carpenters will rough-in a project, then use milled wood parts purchased from a manufacturer to complete the job. Renderings, such as those in Fig. 6-17A and B, are typical of the materials available to modern day woodworkers.

Fig. 6-15A. Carpenter miter cutting wood moulding with a frame and trim saw.
COURTESY OF DELTA INTERNATIONAL MACHINERY CORP.

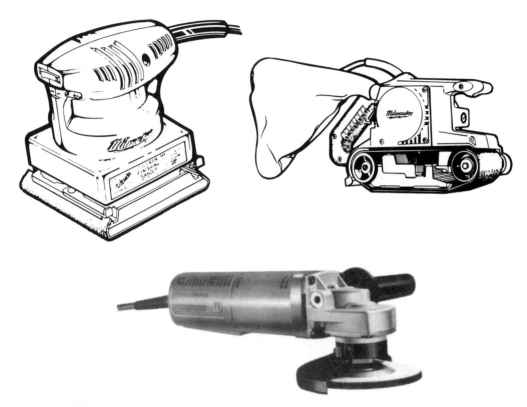

Fig. 6-15B. Belt and orbital sanders. COURTESY OF MILWAUKEE ELECTRIC TOOL CORP., BROOKFIELD, WI 53005.

Fig. 6-16. Vacuum cleaner motor head with 55 gallon drum adapter. COURTESY OF MILWAUKEE ELECTRIC TOOL CORP., BROOK-FIELD, WI 53005.

Fig. 6-17A. Cabinet maker planning mantel trim. COURTESY OF MORGAN PRODUCTS, LTD.

Fig. 6-17B. Assortment of newels and balusters. COURTESY OF MORGAN PRODUCTS, LTD.

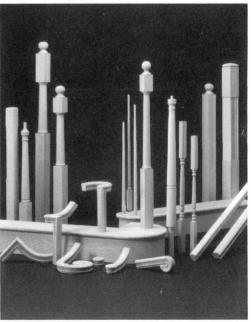
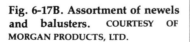

7

Ings and Other Things

YOU SAY YOU DON'T KNOW YOUR SHEETING FROM YOUR SHEATHING? A BANISter from a baluster? I can relate to that. Do you feel the workmen are all perverted when you overhear them referring to cripple studs, bastard files, P-traps, hips, and shakes? You're not alone. It's easy to get lost in construction jargon. Let me assure you, the terms are real. To help you better understand the more common ones, I've created a lexicon of sorts for you to refer to. So the next time you visit a job site and trip over a sleeper or become overwhelmed by all the rabbets and dados, here's a little ken from Ken to ease you through the trauma. Before I begin; balusters are the small posts that hold up the banister, which is the stair railing—just thought you'd want to know.

Bastard File. It has nothing at all to do with legitimacy; a bastard is a rough-cut file or rasp that is flat on one side and half-round on the other.

Bearing Wall. This wall is not a seawall in the Bering Strait; a bearing wall is any wall that bears the weight or load of the structures above it; as opposed to a curtain wall that supports only its own weight.

Bonding. My son says "Bonding is when you pretend you're a spy," but I know for a fact that in masonry it's the pattern chosen by a bricklayer to lock together two or more parts of a structure; the adhesive force existing between mortar and the stones, bricks, or blocks to which it is applied.

Bracing. The scrap metal in my daughter's mouth that amounts to $2,000. In a building, it's the installation of diagonal members between joists, at mid span, to stabilize it against lateral loading; also called bridging or blocking.

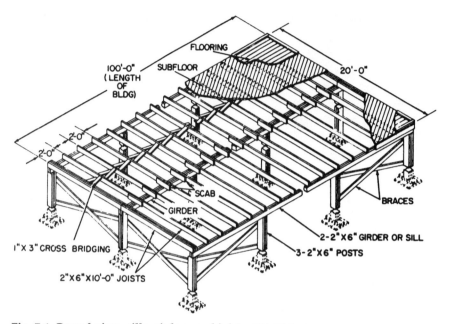

Fig. 7-1. Braced piers, sills, girders, and joists. COURTESY OF BUREAU OF NAVAL PERSONNEL.

Caisson. Caissons, as we go rolling along, are concrete pillars that extend down through poor quality soil and rest on an underlying stratum of rock to provide support to the structures built upon them.

Casing. If you catch someone "casing the joint," that simply means you've caught them applying the wood-finish pieces surrounding a window or door.

Caulking Gun. A caulking gun, pronounced "cocking gun," is simply a device used to apply a variety of sealants to the cracks and crevices around windows, plumbing fixtures, etc.

Cripple Stud. Obviously not what the term implies, cripple studs are short-framing members cut to fit between wall studs above and below windows, and between headers and top plates above door openings.

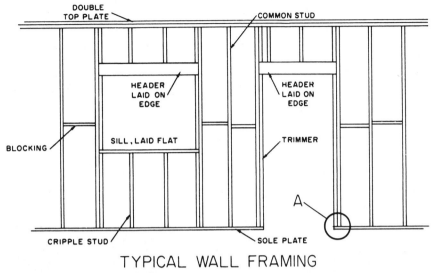

TYPICAL WALL FRAMING

Fig. 7-2. Typical wall framing showing cripple studs above window and door headers and below window sill. COURTESY OF BUREAU OF NAVAL PERSONNEL.

Curing. Though a concrete worker might be able to alleviate your driveway ills, the only curing he causes is when his concrete sets. *Curing* is the planned hardening of substances resulting from the evaporation of the fluids they contain.

Dado. I knew you were curious! A *dado* is a rectangular groove cut into the side of one board to allow for the insertion of a second board.

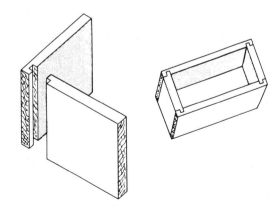

Fig. 7-3. Dado and rabbet joint. COURTESY OF BUREAU OF NAVAL PERSONNEL.

Daylighting. Daylighting, unlike moonlighting, is not the working of a second job during the daytime. It is the illumination of a building's interior by natural means.

Dead Load. If you hear the workers grumbling from time to time about the *dead load*, don't immediately take offense; they're probably referring to the weight of the building.

Feathering. When a drywaller feathers your nest, he's applying multiple coats of joint compound over the seams in your walls, making each successive pass wider and thinner in order to limit the amount of sanding necessary during the finishing process.

Fig. 7-4. Horizontally laid drywall sheets showing feathered-out seams.

Flame Spread. Some of us might be fooled into believing this is a new chili sauce just recently marketed. But, those in the know will tell you that *flame spread* is a value assigned materials that is a measurement of how rapidly fire will spread across surfaces, once ignited.

Flashing. Don't even think about it. *Flashing* is sheet metal, usually galvanized to withstand the elements. It is used to line roof joints around chimneys and vents and prevents water from seeping under the shingles laid around them.

Floating. Come back down here. *Floating* is just the process of smoothing the surface of newly poured concrete by vibrating the larger aggregate or stones to a lower level in the mix.

Footing. Footing is something you want to be damned cognizant of when walking through an unfinished structure. But, for purposes of defining it, *footing* is a mass of concrete located below the frost line on which the foundation is set.

Fig. 7-5. Footing reinforcement installed and awaiting concrete.

Foundation. Contrary to what others might attempt, it would be inappropriate to encourage your friends to donate to your masonry foundation. The sole function of a building's foundation is to transmit the structures loading into the ground.

Framing. No one even pointed a finger at you, let alone accused you of anything. Get real. *Framing* is the active construction of a building's floors, walls, ceilings, and roof. The bones of the skeleton, if you will.

Frost Line. Nope; not a cold call made by a walk-in salesman. The *frost line* is the depth into the ground where the warmth of the soil is sufficient to prevent freezing or the formation of frost.

Fig. 7-6. Newly installed bay type window.

Glazing. In a manner of speaking, you can say it's the icing on the cake, but in reality it's the installation of window glass in its frames.

Grading. You might form an opinion on how good a job the excavator does, but it'll be him that will do the grading. *Grading* is the manipulation of ground soil with earth-moving equipment to bring its surface to a specified level.

Hip. I'm not going to dignify that remark with a response. A *hip* is the external angle formed where two slopes of a roof meet.

Molding. Aside from what you'll start doing if you don't get out of that armchair on occasion, *molding* is decorative or ornamental trim in the form of wood or plastic strips that are applied to walls at the floor and ceiling levels.

Mullion. Did you say ten times a hundred thousand? *Mullions* are the vertical frames separating doors or windows, which are part of the same assembly.

Nosing. No, it's not the opposite of minding your own business; it's the rounded projected edge of a step in a staircase or strip molding at the top of wainscoting or decorative surfaces on cabinetry.

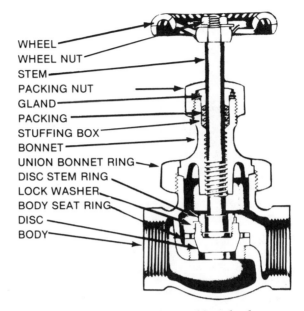

WHEEL
WHEEL NUT
STEM
PACKING NUT
GLAND
PACKING
STUFFING BOX
BONNET
UNION BONNET RING
DISC STEM RING
LOCK WASHER
BODY SEAT RING
DISC
BODY

Fig. 7-7. Cross section of globe valve showing packing gland. COURTESY OF BUILDING OWNERS AND MANAGERS INSTITUTE.

Orientation. Some might say it's knowing where you're going, others, knowing where you are. The fact is, it's the physical placement of a house relative to the points on a compass.

P-trap. Naughty, naughty. A *P-trap* is a plumber's fitting configured in the shape of a P. It is located between a plumbing fixture and its drain line. It maintains a water seal within itself to keep sewage gases out of the house.

Packing. The drudgery you'll be going through if and when they ever finish building the house, you say? No sir. It's loosely packed waterproof material installed in the packing boxes of valves to prevent leakage from occurring around their stems.

Pointing. A ritual that builders and architects go through when things don't go the way they planned, or the application of mortar to finish or repair the surface of a joint after the masonry has been laid.

Rabbet. Not Bugs Bunny. It's a rectangular groove cut along the edge of a piece of wood to accommodate the joining of a second piece of wood.

Fig. 7-8. Bathtub water lines with valves roughed in between wall studs.

Riser. Someone that's up for it; a riser can refer to a vertical run of plumbing, wiring, or ductwork, or the vertical boards closing the spaces between the treads in a staircase.

Roughing-in. Sure, it might be construed as pushing your way in at the job site, but it is really the installation of plumbing, electrical and mechanical lines, and fixtures that aren't normally exposed to view once a project is finished.

Shakes. I know, I know, what you're going to order with your fries. Get serious. *Shakes* are roofing shingles that are hand-hewn from heartwood giving them a rough, textured appearance.

Sheathing. You mean sheeting? *Sheathing* is the rough outer skin that is applied to the exterior of the roof, floor, or wall of a framed structure.

Sheeting. You mean sheathing? *Sheeting* is the material used to retain soil around an excavation.

Sleeper. I hadn't thought about it, but I suppose it's possible this book could be a sleeper. At the moment though, I would be more inclined to consider a sleeper a timber or beam laid horizontally on the ground that is used to support something above it.

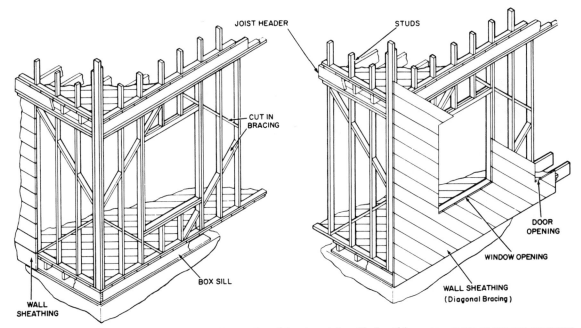

Fig. 7-9. Exterior wall framing showing diagonal and horizontal wall sheathing. COURTESY OF BUREAU OF NAVAL PERSONNEL.

Test Boring. You might find it that way, but it's important that a sample is taken of the soil upon which you intend to build to determine how much weight it is capable of accommodating.

Venting. To some folks it means getting something off their chests; to a mechanic, it's the vertical piping extending through the roof that ventilates the plumbing system or the louvered attic opening under the roof eave that lets the house breathe.

Watt-Hour Meter. What hour meter? It's a device installed by the electrical utility company for tracking the amount of electricity consumed by the household.

Weephole. I empathize with you, but it's not the hole in your pocket you cry through after the builder takes all of your money. It's a small opening along the bottom of a building's exterior used to drain away the water accumulated within its walls.

Fig. 7-10. Watt-hour meter. COURTESY OF WESTINGHOUSE ELECTRIC CORPORATION.

8

The Voice of Experience

As a consequence of my management career, I've supervised over a hundred building renovation and construction projects. Like the people who came together to enact them, each project was identifiable by their individual strengths and foibles. No project can help but take on the character of those charged with its completion. Hopefully, each subsequent endeavor is made better by the insight derived from the last. It's your house; you provide the character. My contribution will be the enlightenment I gained from repeated exposure to the process. What you are is what you produce. Contemplate these points before beginning production.

ASSESSING YOUR NEEDS

By *your* needs, I am referring less to you individually than to your family on the whole. Before workable decisions can be made regarding a home's functionality, the requirements of all persons who will be effected must first be considered.

- Will you be keeping the house for a lifetime or do you plan on selling it some years down the road?
- How many people will be living there? What are their ages? Sexes?
- If one of the family members is handicapped, can counters, fixtures, and control switches be lowered without undue hardship to the rest of the clan?

- Do you want a formal dining room, an informal one adjacent to the living room, or will you eat in the kitchen?
- How much company does the household receive? What about overnight guests and vacationers?
- Is there more than one worker in the family? Is an office in the home needed? Two? How private?
- What space is needed for activities? How much entertaining goes on? Do parties usually get rowdy?
- Are there any artists, collectors, or hobbyists in the group? Did you look into natural lighting? Extra shelving? Cabinets? A workshop?
- Where are you going to keep the lawn tractor and garden tools?

ATTACKING THE LAYOUT

I'll buy the idea that homes are meant to be lived in. I'll even go as far as to agree that it isn't necessary to keep everything neat as a pin and in its place, 100 percent of the time. But, I'm inflexible when it comes to the functional layout of a structure. It just won't do to have people physically bumping into one another, interfering with each other's activities, or enduring intrusions into their private spaces. It's important to get it right from the start; take these thoughts into consideration and think through your options.

- There should be plenty of space in a room, and its shape should be right to accommodate the activities that will occur there.
- Sufficient clearance around furniture and appliances enables two people to pass each other comfortably.
- Locate windows in front of the scenes you want to view, at the same time, allowing for alternate furniture arrangements.
- Doors should open into rooms by the normal way of travel. Closet doors should never open into hallways.
- Halls waste space. A central foyer opening into several rooms might be preferable.
- Multipurpose rooms might be considered when confronted with a small budget and a diverse list of possible uses.
- You might want to split the plan and put your children's bedrooms on another floor or the other side of the house.
- Traffic flow within a room should make sense to the work performed there.
- Avoid low overheads and too-high shelves in cabinetry and storage rooms.
- In northern climes, air locks used at entrances conserve precious energy and double as mudrooms during periods of inclement weather.

- In rooms where a tight squeeze is anticipated, consider installing decorative chair rails on the walls.
- Where acoustics are important have double-studded insulated walls installed and utilize heavy drapes, carpet, and/or acoustical materials.
- If space is a limiting factor, you might want to install pass-throughs in a wall that can be closed-in with shutters when not in use.
- Be cognizant of the infiltration of sunlight into a room during the day or roadway lights from traffic at night.
- The laundry room should be large enough to iron in and contain space for hanging ironed clothes and storing linen.
- A bathroom should be located in close proximity to recreation and activity areas that open onto the patio.
- Mechanicals should be hidden from obvious view, and their rooms never used for storage.
- Locate fireplaces so that no surface or person within 5 feet of the opening is subject to its radiant heat.
- Consider only walk-in closets. You never have enough storage space.

BELAYING FUTURE MAINTENANCE

You've probably heard this a thousand times before, but "it costs more to fix it than to do it right the first time." Nowhere is this adage more often manifested than after a house has been built using shoddy materials or poor workmanship. Two other truisms you might take to heart; "the dollar you save now might well cost you ten later," and "if you want to save a few bucks, you have to spend a few." Listen up!

- A one piece tub and shower will save you from the need to regrout ceramic tile walls and floors.
- Sheet veneers used for wall covering and counters instead of ceramic tile in wet areas cut down on mildew problems.
- "No-wax floors" are just that; no waxing needed. Resilient sheeting also doesn't suffer the problems caused by water to individual vinyl tiles.
- In the North, snow removal is a problem on paved areas; in the South, grass cutting can be a nuisance in unpaved areas.
- The nice thing about brick exteriors is that they don't need painted, though some modern sidings have also all but eliminated the need.
- Use only good quality fixtures, galvanized fasteners, and pressure-treated lumber in wet areas.
- Don't put a window on a tub wall, but do put a curb at the base of a shower to retain the water.

- Never ventilate a bathroom's exhaust into the attic or air return system.
- Use frequent support straps on gutters and downspouts, and screen all open areas to keep out leaves and pests.
- Floor drains should be installed in garages and laundry rooms, and all water should completely drain away from a building.
- No exposed wood should be used in bathrooms, and water supply pipes should not be located on outside walls.
- Sizing applied to all walls receiving wallcoverings allow for quick and easy removal later.

BUILT-INS

It wasn't too long ago that many of our modern conveniences were referred to as contrivances, gadgets, or contraptions and thought to be luxuries that people could really do without, even if they could afford them. Today, not only are they considered necessary, but they've evolved to become an integral part of our everyday existence. What follows isn't a complete list of all possible items you might want to have built into your home, but it should serve to stir up your gray matter concerning the subject.

- Garbage disposals and dishwashers tied into the kitchen sink drain
- Saunas, steam baths, or jacuzzis
- Piggyback washers and dryers
- Self-cleaning ranges with microwave oven or grilling capability
- Exhaust fans for removing dining room smoke, kitchen and bathroom odors, and providing whole house ventilation through the attic
- Accessories such as soap dispensers, towel racks, and paper holders
- Grab bars, and hand and chair railings
- Refrigerated bars complete with sinks, stereos, and televisions
- Trash compactors and appliance garages in the kitchen
- Broom closets and mini desks in the kitchen
- Coat/boot racks and storage bins with seating in the foyer
- Shelving throughout the house

CARPENTRY

Carpentry is probably the most visible aspect of a construction project in its early stages, but the least visible once it's completed. So, before all the other tradesmen cover up (there's that word again) their work, it's a good idea to check on what the carpenter has done. It's logical that problems arising later might well be linked to how good a carpentry job you got earlier, but before you nail the poor guy to the wall, first see if he's given you this.

- Structural members are built on 16 inch centers or better.
- Appropriate grades of wood are chosen for the job on which it is used.
- Woodwork, other than framing, is glued and doweled.
- Additional support is built into structures used to support heavy loading, as from a waterbed or nautilus.
- Stairs are 3 feet wide or better with a center stringer; folding-attic stairs serve no useful purpose whatsoever.
- Subfloor and joist seams should not coincide; underlayment and finish floor panels should overlap.
- Glued dado and rabbet joints should be used instead of nailed butt joints.
- Cathedral ceilings should contain a ridge beam to support the central roof weight.
- Diagonal braces used on all structural walls.
- Screws should be used instead of nails whenever possible.
- All wall openings should be double-studded to reinforce the wall members.
- Strip standards for supporting shelves should be inset and not surface mounted.
- Frequent newels should be placed in stair balustrades to give added stability.
- European hinges are used on all cabinetry doors for better appearance and greater swing.
- Stay away from pocket doors that are recessed into the wall.

COLOR AND GEOMETRY

The aesthetic appeal of a home is dependent on the visual effect produced by the shapes, forms, and colors, as well as the individual likes and dislikes of the observer. I believe it was Abraham Lincoln who first expressed that you can please some of the people some of the time, but never everyone all the time. Ken's rule of observation states that "the number of opinions arrived at concerning the aesthetic appearance of a thing observed is directly proportional to the number of people observing it." In other words, no two people that look at the same object ever come away with exactly the same impression. The verdict isn't in yet on the benefits of hiring interior designer/decorators, but I personally feel that it's your house and, as such, should be a reflection of who you are. Besides, why pay someone good money to come into your home and tell you what you like? You already know that, and what you don't know about the visual effect of patterns, textures, and hues you can learn at your local library. But peruse these pointers before you start looking for your card.

- If you insist on having a hallway, make the walls a light color to visually open it up.
- Dress up a less expensive rectangular-shaped house with bump outs, such as dormers and bay windows.
- Break up the monotony of long straight walls by using vault ceilings, rounded arches, and half partitions.
- Consider how your old furniture will fit the proposed decor.
- Will the rooms swallow up your possessions or bulge as you cram them with too many items for their size?
- Are the textures you've chosen for your wall coverings compatible with what you'll be hanging on them?
- Better to have house extensions such as enclosed patios, sun-rooms and carports built at the same time so that the materials used to construct the roof, walls, and deck or concrete match those on the house.
- Have a barbecue pit built from the same brick used on the house.
- Materials such as carpeting and wallcoverings should come from the same run; other items such as bricks or floor tile can come from different batches but must be thoroughly mixed before being set in place.

CONCRETE AND MASONRY

Are you one of those people who frequently use the terms concrete and cement interchangeably? They aren't the same, you know. Strictly speaking, cement is actually the glue used to make concrete. It is generally accepted as being a powdered substance made of burned lime and clay that is mixed with water and sand to make mortar and to sand, water, and gravel to make concrete. Concrete then, is a solid mass produced by a combination of ingredients, including cement. I thought I'd share that with you, since your home will literally be based on concrete. Here are some ditties having to do with them both, and the bricks and stones they hold in place.

- Make sure that the minimum thickness of the concrete mix prescribed is always met.
- Slump tests should be performed before each pour to determine the consistency of the mix.
- Concrete splash plates located at the base of downspout leaders direct water away from buildings, eliminating soil erosion.

- Whenever possible, avoid pouring large concrete masses during time periods when the outdoor temperature approaches freezing.
- Don't allow heavy loads to be applied to freshly set concrete, such as when fully loaded trucks are driven over a new walk.
- Consider using colored concrete in heavy-traffic recreational areas.
- Brick, block, or stone walls located near roadways dampen street noises and provide visual privacy.
- Types, colors, textures, and patterns of brick, block, and stone can set the mood for the areas where they are used.
- Concrete edging should be rounded to reduce chipping and cracking.
- Wire mesh and reinforcing rods must be properly suspended to position them at the correct level within the concrete.
- A mortared brick or stone walk is best placed on a concrete pad to keep the units from settling and the mortar from cracking.
- The cost to build a finished basement is less per square foot than for construction of the floors above it.
- Make certain that concrete cure time is strictly adhered to.
- Concrete should always be placed on a bed of gravel, and forms should be removed just after the concrete sets up.
- Control joints should be placed every twenty feet in brick and/or block walls to minimize cracking caused by temperature changes.
- Brick, block, and stone walls held together by mortar should be cleaned with an acid solution when they're completed.

ELECTRICAL CONCERNS

It's been said that electricity is not a science but a theory. We know less about what electricity is than the effects it produces. On a practical level, it is the stuff of life; a substance which, at once, we both fear and take for granted. The awesome power possessed of electrical current need not be feared but must certainly be respected by all who are responsible for its generation, transmission, and consumption. The National Electrical Code (NEC), in conjunction with the progressive efforts of associations such as Underwriters Laboratory (UL) and the National Electrical Manufacturers Association (NEMA) help assure the safety of us all in its distribution and use. Keep your eye on the electricians, but don't give them any static until you've checked on these.

- Ground current fault interrupters (GFCI) in wet areas to trip circuit breakers when you're in imminent danger of electrical shock
- Metal plates placed on studs where wires have been pulled to protect them from nails, screws, and drill bits

- A service entrance large enough to accommodate present as well as future needs
- Spare circuits installed now for fixtures to be installed later, such as exhaust fans, ceiling fans, chandeliers, outdoor security lighting and receptacles, pool heaters . . . etc.
- Emergency lighting circuits either battery powered for lighting or hooked to an autonomous source of power, such as a gas-engine powered generator
- Covers on incandescent lights that can come into contact with moisture, bare skin, or fabric of any kind
- Extra outlets in high-use areas and separate circuits for high current draw devices, such as refrigerators and toaster ovens
- Recessed lighting, dimmer switches, and higher lighting levels in studies and children's bedrooms
- Extra runs of television and telephone cables to allow for easy rearrangements later without cutting into walls and floors

EXCAVATION AND LANDSCAPING

This is where all the physical work begins. Can you dig it? Huh? Sorry about that . . . but you knew it was coming didn't you? I'd have to have a hole in my head to let that one go by. Alright already, don't get down into the pits over it. Here are a couple of items to cite concerning the site.

- Make certain all required tests are performed and properly documented.
- Call for the complete removal of rocks, stumps, and debris.
- Topsoil should be removed to an inactive area for reclaiming after rough grading.
- The footing carrying the foundation walls must extend below the frostline.
- Reuse bushes, trees, and naturally occurring stones whenever possible.
- Consider tiers and retaining walls to thwart erosion.
- Make sure all nicks made in the vapor barrier are repaired, before the barrier is covered over with dirt.

MATERIALS AND HARDWARE

Now is not the time for skimping. If you must cut costs, build a smaller place or do without the swimming pool for now but whatever you do, don't cut back on the quality of materials used to construct your palace or the hardware with which it will be embellished. Remember, there's a high cost associated with cheap construction. As you're making your selections, keep these thoughts in mind.

- Natural heartwood or galvanized sheet metal shields can keep carpenter ants and termites from setting up house in your home.
- Carpet and/or wood floors are a poor choice for kitchens, bathrooms, and other areas exposed to moisture.
- Carpeting and floor and wallcoverings should be made of materials that will withstand the abuse doled out to them.
- Underlayment for resilient flooring and padding for carpeting are standard.
- Gutters are a must to direct water away from your house, but have them installed so they won't cause problems later from freeze-thaw cycling.
- Accept only high-grade caulking, glazing, and sealing compounds.
- Use seamless floors or bare-colored concrete in wet areas.
- Never specify butcher block for an entire counter, rather have a lay-in cutting surface installed.
- Keep acoustics in mind when selecting decorative materials.
- Use only top of the line hardware such as Euro hinges on the kitchen cabinets.
- Watch out for "or equal" substitutions.
- Use textured materials to avoid frequent cleaning of fingerprints from surfaces.
- No murals, cheap hardware, or decorative paper on light switches and receptacles.
- Arrange for the return of all unused materials minus the amount needed for future repairs.

MECHANICALS AND PLUMBING

Throughout the confines of our homes are located devices that mother us with comfort, convenience, and security. Our hollow walls are lined with their metal conduits, not unlike umbilical cords, connecting them to us. We've grown accustomed to their unwavering daily operation, except for the infrequent outages we suffer at the hands of our utility companies. When properly installed, today's mechanicals are cost-effective, maintenance-free extensions of ourselves that provide us with continuous, reliable service. Because we all should enjoy the trouble-free operation associated with the professional installation of quality equipment, I've compiled these pointers just for you.

- Pay specific attention to where diffusers and return air grilles are placed.

- Manage heating and cooling by zones, and locate thermostats in the areas they will serve.
- Augment bathroom heat with a radiant, electrical resistance heater located in the ceiling.
- Consider the use of a heat pump if the climate is conducive to its utilization.
- Using humidifiers in winter and dehumidifiers in summer with fans help lower cooling and heating loads.
- No air return grille should be located in a high-moisture area feeding back into the main air system.
- Buy only top of the line washerless plumbing fixtures and have compression fittings installed in place of soldered joints whenever possible.
- All chimneys and vent pipes extending beyond the roof should be screened and capped.
- Water softeners remove scaling salts that can cause fouling of water heaters, pipes, and appliances.
- All water-carrying pipes must be pitched to avoid air entrapment, and air bleeders should be installed at the highest points in hot water heating systems.
- Generously sized panels should be installed to enable quick and easy access to conduits and valves for repairs.
- Energy can be conserved through the use of flow restrictors in shower heads.
- Utility meters should be located on the outside of the home for the convenience of the meter reader.
- Water heaters should be sized to produce enough hot water for two people to take showers, back to back, while a wash is being done.
- Water inlet lines need to be sized large enough to avoid significant pressure drops when multiple taps are open in the system at the same time.
- The best bet in a water heater is one that recovers quickly, is energy efficient, and comes with an exterior wrap of insulation.
- Shut-off valves at each plumbing fixture enables the isolation of individual fixtures without shutting down the entire system.
- Dishwashers should discharge directly through the garbage disposal to keep any remaining foodstuffs from entering the drainage system whole.

SAFETY AND SECURITY

Nowhere in the world should you feel more safe and secure than in your own home. Cops can be crooked, national guardsmen are sometimes scary by themselves, and you'll leave your lover before you'll ever think of leaving your home. What's the first thing you think of when you're cold, wet, and tired while out in the elements? Where do you want to be when you find yourself in a strange place or confronted with danger? Need I say more? Take care of your home by heeding the advice in these blurbs and, your home will take care of you.

- Lightning rods provide obvious protection against fire caused by strikes to the structure.
- Cut down large trees located too closely to your home or its incoming power source.
- Window curtains in close proximity to open heaters are an invitation for fire.
- Rooms where batteries are stored for emergency lighting during power outages should be vented to prevent the accumulation of combustible gases.
- Flue liners protect encased surrounding structures from the heat it contains in the chimney.
- Substantial window locks and dead bolts on steel doors provide security against intruders.
- Handrails and grab bars provide the added stability sometimes needed by old or infirm people.
- Fire walls placed between mechanical rooms or garages and the main body of the house slow the spread of flame through the structure.
- Fire extinguishers located in the kitchen, garage, and mechanical rooms can save the destruction of your home if properly used when needed.
- Having all locks keyed alike eliminates fumbling for keys and makes lock changes easier and less expensive.
- Open flames indoors consume large quantities of oxygen that should be acquired from the outside atmosphere.
- Plastic used in place of glass, in the bath, limits the harm it can do when it's broken.
- Nonskid surfaces in wet areas provide a safer footing, thereby limiting the number of falls encountered.
- Mixing valves on water taps, having preset temperatures, protect against scalding.
- Bathroom doors that can be unlocked from the outside allow entry for medical emergencies.
- A step-up curb located by the house entrance from the garage keeps carbon monoxide gases from flowing along the floor to your pet or baby.
- Glass block walls offer the security of solid construction while still allowing the infiltration of light into the space.

- Walls and fences are physical obstructions to trespassers and well-placed exterior lighting adds to the visual security.
- Antennae, located near power lines that are unprotected by lightning rods, become lightning rods.
- Fireproof buildings located away from the main house are a good place to provide storage for all household combustibles.
- Stairs that are sloped other than standard pose a tripping hazard.
- Retractable electrical cords in hobby and work areas are automatically stored and pose no tripping hazards.
- Three-way switches at landings make light constantly available while traversing the staircase.
- Pins inserted in door stiles that fit into the jambs when the doors are locked keep them in place when the hinges are removed.
- Door closers on fire doors provide automatic closure and latching of doors when they are left open.
- A lockable cabinet having a door closer is an excellent place to store caustic or poisonous substances away from children.
- Many household accidents can be avoided simply by supplying the appropriate amount of light for the task being performed.
- Snow guards on roofs over doorways prevent accumulations of ice and snow from falling onto the people under them.

SAVING MONEY

Whether dollars have just lost their punch or we simply don't have them to spread around, one thing is certain. Like any finite resource, the less we conserve our money the poorer we will be. When having a home built, it's imperative that you keep that at the forefront of your mind. Otherwise you can very easily end up house poor. So, review your budget twice prior to pulling out your bankbook and these items thrice before filling out the checks.

- Build only for now and the immediate future, but plan the layout to make add-ons easier later.
- Eliminate the formal dining room and eat in the family room or kitchen.
- Use local occurring rock and vegetation to keep landscaping costs down.
- The season and a builder's schedule both have a bearing on the cost of construction.
- Multilevel houses are cheaper to build than one-story houses having the same square footage due to less excavation, footing, and foundation work.

- An attached garage is cheaper to build than a detached one due to the common wall it shares with the house.
- The least expensive designs are the simplest having the plainest configurations, such as square or rectangular shapes.
- Money can be saved by using stock material that is locally produced of the lowest grade that will still do the job.
- Flat clear plots of land cost less to grade than overgrown hilly ground.
- It's cheaper to have a house constructed where nearby utilities already exist.
- Using prefabricated sections and prefinished materials, such as pre-hung doors or milled woodwork reduces labor costs.
- Thermopane or evacuated double and triple-pane windows increase energy efficiency and reduce heating bills.
- Factory-built chimneys reduce labor costs, and their dampers reduce energy costs.
- Savings can be had by minimizing custom-built items and avoiding change orders on standard items.
- Money can be saved if your builder agrees to let you perform the interior trash removal, painting, or other work.
- Dimension building takes advantage of the standard material sizes and all but eliminates the cost of waste.
- Money can be saved if a second or third bath is limited to a water closet and sink or having a shower stall installed in place of a tub.
- Using a cluster wall for plumbing lowers labor costs, and using standard plumbing fixtures and parts saves on repairs.
- Shade trees and skylights not only add character and splendor to your home, but they each contribute to energy savings when properly utilized.
- Insulate your walls, roof, and floors; insulate your water heater, pipes, and ducts.
- The elimination of hallways allows for more productive use of built space.
- Creative use of dead space under stairs, in the attic and basement effectively increases living space and lowers the cost of building.
- An additional stall built into the garage provides relatively inexpensive space for work and hobby activities or storage.

9

Home Building Specifications

DETERMINING WHAT MATERIALS AND TECHNIQUES WILL BE USED IN THE CONstruction of your home can be similar to a search for a good spouse. And, just as a marriage based on superficial virtues is doomed to failure, so will a house suffer a premature demise if it's made of less than substantial stuff. Years ago, it was enough for an aroused young man to pine for ". . . a girl, just like the girl that married dear old Dad." These days, unless of course he's an utter masochist, he needs to be more realistic about her qualifications. Likewise, if a house is to last a lifetime, more stringent specifications must be used in its construction than someone pointing to a brochure and stating "I want one just like that one."

The following is typical of specification documents you'll find in the home building industry. Its presence here is meant to jog your thinking on the subject; not prescribe the methods and materials to be used on your particular project. And, while I'm qualifying the textual intent of the information contained in this chapter, please don't interpret my allusions to marriage as a condescending indictment against the virtues of women or motherhood; I realize that we men are just as human. Nevertheless, even if you choose to ignore my creative imaging of the subject, be sure to take the time to review this descriptive specification sampling. Understanding this process can save you a great deal of money and grief.

GENERAL CONDITIONS

The general conditions normally precede the technical portion of the specification instrument. In this section, the project's principals are named as they will be referred to later in the document, and their general responsibilities are stated. The codes to which the project must adhere can be spelled out, and the terminology used throughout the instrument defined.

Example:

1. Definitions

    a) Whenever the word "Owner" is used herein, it means (your name).

    b) Whenever the word "Builder" is used herein, it means the individual or firm (x y z Company) undertaking to do all of the work called for in the contract.

    c) Whenever the word "Architect" or "Engineer" is used herein, it means the architect or engineer engaged by and acting on behalf of the owner.

    d) Whenever the word "Subcontractor" is used herein, it refers to the individual or firm having a direct contract with and who is answerable to the Builder.

    e) Whenever the word "acceptable" or "approved" is used herein, it means the material or work shall be acceptable to or approved by the Owner.

2. Intent

    a) The drawings and specifications, with the contract, are intended to provide and comprise everything necessary for the thorough completion of the project.

    b) Should any error be found or any doubt exist regarding the true intent and/or meaning of the drawings or specifications, the Builder shall immediately apply to the Architect or Engineer, as appropriate, for correction or explanation thereof. But in all cases, the Owner has the final say involving any dispute.

3. Builder's Responsibility

    a) The Builder shall provide sufficient safeguards to thwart the occurrence of accidents to all persons on the property of the owner.

b) The Builder is responsible to ensure that all work is performed using only the prescribed materials, applied with a high standard of workmanship, acceptable to the building industry.

c) The Builder shall be responsible for all damages caused by his operations to all parts of the work and any adjoining property.

4. Subcontractors

a) The Builder will contract separately with all subcontractors he uses to substitute his operation.

b) All subcontractors will answer directly to the Builder concerning all aspects of material acquisition, transportation, set-up, work scheduling, and clean-up.

c) The final approval of all subcontractors, used by the Builder, rests with the Owner.

5. Poor Workmanship

a) Recourse for poor or untimely workmanship or the failure of materials to meet specification will be spelled out in the main body of the contract.

6. Owner Inspections

a) The Owner or his authorized representative shall at all times be welcome at the site and given reasonable access to the work being performed there.

7. Substitutions

a) The Owner has the exclusive right of acceptance and/or approval of any substitutions to that prescribed in the specifications document.

8. Codes and Standards

a) All project work, regardless of who performs it, must conform to all applicable standards required by the building code adopted in the contract, adhere to the municipal ordinances in which the residence is to be located, and comply with the legitimate recommendations made by any inspector, based on his findings, as they relate to the law or code from which he derives his authority.

GENERAL REQUIREMENTS

Any requirement not expressly addressed in the body of the contract, that does not otherwise qualify as a specification or condition, falls into this category. General requirements can include anything from the building of a temporary road to access the job site, to limiting the amount of noise or dirt that can be produced there.

Example:

1. Meetings and Reports

   a) A regularly scheduled weekly progress meeting will be held by the builder to report on the status and direction of the work. It can be attended by any or all of the project's principals.

   b) Each week a progress report will be prepared by the Builder, for the Owner, listing any problems he had and how they were resolved.

2. Temporary Facilities

   a) All temporary facilities including electricity, lighting, water, sewage, HVAC, telephone and sanitation, if required by the Builder, shall be installed at his own expense.

   b) The Builder shall install a first-aid station near the building site to provide for the emergency care of visitors receiving injuries there.

3. System & Equipment Integrity

   a) Each system and system component must be installed per manufacturers guidelines, tested in place, and adjusted until it performs to its intended design.

   b) The Builder will supply the Owner with reports of all tests performed on the Owner's equipment and systems, as well as any operating manuals and warranty information that accompanies the equipment as received from the manufacturer.

SITE WORK

Generally, site work specifications determine how the site itself will be prepared to accommodate the construction that will follow, what site improvements will be made, how utilities are to be accessed, and addresses reclamation of the land after completion of the building process.

Example:

1. Clearing

   a) Remove all trees and bushes from the entire lot, boxing those designated by the owner for replanting later.

   b) Stockpile all existing topsoil for later reclaiming, remove stumps, and debris to a separate area for hauling.

2. Excavation

   a) Excavate for footing under main structure to a depth indicated at the corners, and stockpile extruded material for backfilling later.

   b) Stake out septic area and outbuildings.

   c) Trench out for underground utilities to prescribed depth, install conduits, and backfill.

3. Grading

   a) Cut in the drives and walkways and finish-grade the remaining areas to the plan.

   b) Provide erosion control as required and install culverts at the mid and end points of the drive to facilitate storm water drainage.

4. Driveway Base

   a) A base composed of bank gravel or similar material to be installed to a leveled depth of ten inches when compacted, then dressed with limestone for acceptance of a finish surface.

CONCRETE AND MASONRY

Obviously, this section deals with the brick, block, and mortar used to support and construct the building, its facade, and the ways of travel leading from it.

Example:

1. Concrete Basis

   a) All concrete form and finish work will comply with local building code requirements.

   b) Only washed gravel and silica sand can be used in the mix.

   c) All finished concrete must be maintained within 1/4 inch of level and square.

2. Footings

   a) House footings shall be 24 × 10 inches thick, made with air-entrained ASTM Type I—3000 psi general purpose concrete with two #4 continuous reinforcement.

   b) Garage footings shall be 16 × 8 inches subject to the same specifications as the house footings.

3. Other Concrete

   a) All slabs will be made of 3500 psi reinforced with wire mesh over a 4-inch base of wash gravel troweled to a smooth finish.

   b) All other walkway surfaces shall conform to slab specs except that they will be broom finished.

   c) Driveway will be blacktopped.

4. Masonry

   a) Foundation and basement walls shall be built using 8-inch blocks with wire wall reinforcement on 16-inch centers.

   b) Bricks shall be moistened before being laid and mortar joints to be tooled concave.

   c) Steel lintels shall be installed above all wall openings.

   d) All masonry walls will be acid cleaned after completion.

CARPENTRY

The carpentry section covers an endless variety of materials from two basic vantage points; rough and finish work.

Example:

1. Rough

   a) Exterior walls to be constructed of 2×6s and interior walls of 2×4s.

   b) All walls and joists to be on 16-inch centers and plumb within $1/4$ inch.

   c) Double joists are to be used under all structures having more than ordinary weight placed on them.

   d) All joists shall be crossbridged at midspan to stabilize the floors above them.

   e) All sheathing shall be $1/2$ inch and installed vertically with sheathing nails every twelve inches along the studs.

2. Finish

   a) All exposed beams, moulding, and chair rail are to be made of select oak as set out in the drawings.

   b) Built-in shelving in the den, laundry room, and all closets shall be made of select grade B or better with exterior access doors and jambs of oak veneers.

   c) Stair treads and risers to be constructed of $3/4$-inch plywood with oak veneer; Newels, balusters, and handrail will be solid oak.

   d) All exterior deck work shall be of wolmanized lumber per drawing.

THERMAL AND MOISTURE PROTECTION

T and M protection entails the use of sealants and vapor barriers to eliminate the infiltration of moisture into a building's interior, insulation to keep hot and cold air on the right side of the structure, roofing materials to keep out the rain and fireproofing measures, and materials and methods.

Example:

1. Moisture Proofing

   a) Single coat foundation walls with approved waterproofing sealer, then cover completely with visqueen of no less than 6 mil gauge before backfilling.

b) The entire perimeter of the house is to receive a footing drain consisting of perforated PVC piping nested in six inches of gravel that discharges to grade.

c) Roofing materials shall consist of #15 asphalt saturated felt stapled to plywood deck and 30 year fiberglass shingles attached with galvanized roofing nails.

2. Thermal Protection

a) R-19 or better insulation batts will be placed in basement and exterior walls; R-30 or better in attic.

b) All interior sides shall include a vapor barrier of no less than 6-mil visqueen; free of rips and gaps.

c) All ductwork and piping to be insulated according to the schedules located in the drawings.

d) Caulking around window and door openings shall be as specified in drawing notes.

3. Fireproofing

a) All finish materials used will have a flame spread of B or better as outlined in the architect's recommendations section, and firestopping is to be installed per the blueprint details.

DOORS AND WINDOWS

Obviously, what's covered here are door and window selections, the methods by which they are installed, and their sealing and weatherstripping. Specifications tend to be very brand specific.

Example:

1. Doors

a) All doors and assemblies will be as indicated in the door schedule attached to the drawings.

b) Only (x brand) of doors with solid brass accessories and oak veneers to match the interior wood work will be acceptable.

c) Only (y brand) locks with extended dead bolts will be acceptable.

d) All doors shall be keyed alike.

e) Compatible screens will be provided for all storm doors.

2. Windows

a) All windows and assemblies shall be as indicated in the window schedule attached to the drawings.

b) Only (x brand) of windows and hardware is to be used.

c) Glass is to be tinted in the locations so indicated.

d) Every window shall come equipped with removable storm windows and screens.

FINISHES

Generally, the materials used for finishing a house's interior floors, walls, and ceilings fall into this category; including special coatings and acoustical treatment.

Example:

1. Drywall

a) No less than $5/8$-inch will be glued and screwed throughout.

b) All ceilings will be patterned per owner's choice of design as discussed with plasterer.

c) Double overlapping sheets shall be installed on common wall connecting the garage and house.

d) All joints are to be taped, three coated, and sanded smooth.

e) All interior walls are to be sized to accept vinyl coverings.

f) All outside corners shall receive metal beading strips.

2. Wallcoverings

a) All wallcoverings are to be of the gauge spelled out in the drawing notation for that location and shall be in accordance with the owner's selection only.

3. Floorcoverings

a) Only single sheet resilient vinyl floorcoverings, with underlayment, are acceptable in wet areas.

b) Wall-to-wall carpeting will be provided with a full size pad that extends into closet spaces.

c) Carpeting is to be installed to tack strips around room perimeters.

d) No floor seams are to be visible, and thresholds are to be installed where floorcoverings end at wall openings.

FURNISHINGS

Furnishings are items that dress up or make a home's interior functional. They include manufactured cabinetry, furniture and accessories, fabrics selected for draperies, rugs and mats, and even the artwork that will hang on the wall.

Example:

1. Cabinets

   a) All kitchen cabinets and bathroom vanities are to be purchased from (x brand) per owner's prior selection only.

   b) Cabinets are to be purchased without hardware, as Euro-hinges and handles have been purchased separately, to be installed by (y company) after cabinets have been hung.

2. Carpeting

   a) See Finishes.

3. Window Treatment

   a) All rods, drapes, and curtains will be only as selected; Owner must be notified before any substitutions are made.

MECHANICAL

Probably the most comprehensive in the specification document, the mechanical section covers all the materials and methods used for installing, supporting, and operating every physical device, component of system, other than electric, found in the home. It covers the areas of HVAC, plumbing, fire-suppression, air distribution, and more.

Example:

1. Plumbing

    a) All water supply lines are to be type L rigid copper.

    b) The water supply main will be ³/₄ inch.

    c) No plumbing or venting can be concealed before receiving the inspector's approval on its installation.

2. HVAC

    a) All heating, ventilation, and air-conditioning equipment shall be installed according to the locations and notations in the mechanical pages of the drawings.

3. Controls and Instrumentation

    a) Each floor is to be zoned and thermostats are to be located such that the relative comfort of an individual in any given area can not be compromised by a person controlling another zone or area.

    b) Smoke dampers with automatic resets to be located at all wall penetrations.

    c) Heat and smoke detectors to be hard wired into the air distribution system.

ELECTRICAL

Last on the list but possibly first in importance, is the electrical section that involves the selection of materials and methods used for installing electrical systems and components. This section addresses the issues of power generation, transmission and distribution, lighting, communications, and other electricity-dependent items.

Example:

1. Power Generation

    a) An autonomous gasoline fired (x brand) engine driving a (y brand) electrical generator will be installed through an automatic power loss transfer switch per the drawings supplied by the engineer to supply emergency power to selected circuits in the house.

b) A well ventilated battery bank shall be installed per the engineer's drawings to supply emergency lighting in the pool area.

2. Electrical Distribution

a) All circuit breakers located in the 200 ampere service panel will be plainly labeled to indicate the areas they serve.

3. Other

a) A telephone jack and coaxial television cable will be installed in the kitchen, living room, family room, and all the bedrooms.

b) Extra outlets and lighting are to be installed in the garage and family room as indicated by the changes on the drawings.

SUMMING UP

The foregoing are but a sampling of the dictates used to form the body of a specifications instrument. The next one you come across could well contain all or none of those herein mentioned, which are structurally typical of what you will find in a home-building document.

To what extent which areas are addressed is dependent on your needs and wants, applicable local building codes, the thoroughness of the project principals, how much money is involved, and many other factors. The importance of the document doesn't lie with the number of specifications it lists, but in its ability to convey proper and adequate information to those charged with meeting its requirements.

10

Getting What You Paid For

So, YOU SAY THE HOUSE IS FINISHED, AND THEY GAVE YOU THE KEYS TO check it out? Marvelous! Sure, I'll be happy to tag along; that is, if you don't mind me snooping around a little. Before we leave, let's assemble the implements we'll need to give it a good going-over. You see, the house might be considered completed, but your job isn't over until you ascertain that it's been completed properly.

In order for us to perform a thorough inspection, we'll need a flashlight, electrical tester, torpedo level, 25-foot tape measure, stud finder, gloves, screwdriver, an inspection mirror, and a pen to record our findings on the inspection document that makes up the remainder of this chapter. Because there are no guidelines as to how we should proceed through the house, why don't we start at the front door? First, we'll do a walk through of the entire place, noting any discrepancies we find of items common to all areas. After that, we'll make a second pass to check out those things that are more room specific. Then we'll proceed to the outside to inspect the exterior building and grounds.

Walls:

	Room	Room	Room
Out of square	_____	_____	_____
Corners don't meet	_____	_____	_____
Drywall seams show	_____	_____	_____
Trim broken/missing	_____	_____	_____
Gouges in surface	_____	_____	_____
Registers not flush	_____	_____	_____
Wallcovering bubbled	_____	_____	_____
Ripped/wrong	_____	_____	_____
Nails/screws not set	_____	_____	_____
Corner bead dented	_____	_____	_____
Wrong paint/color	_____	_____	_____
Plaster stained	_____	_____	_____
Cracked/flaking	_____	_____	_____
_____	_____	_____	_____
_____	_____	_____	_____
_____	_____	_____	_____

Comments: _____

_____

_____

Floors:

	Room	Room	Room
Floors bowed/out of/	_____	_____	_____
square/squeak/crack	_____	_____	_____
Coverings ripped/loose/	_____	_____	_____
discolored/wrong	_____	_____	_____
Cove base missing	_____	_____	_____
Wrong color/type	_____	_____	_____
Tiles broken/missing	_____	_____	_____
Tile grout loose/missing	_____	_____	_____
_____	_____	_____	_____
_____	_____	_____	_____
_____	_____	_____	_____

Comments: _____

_____

_____

Ceilings:

	Room	Room	Room
Out of square			
Stained/broken/			
missing tiles			
Light fixture broken/			
loose/missing			
Grid strips crooked/			
bent/wrong			
Surface chipped/gouged			
Wrong plaster pattern			

Comments: _____

_____

_____

Doors and Windows:

	Room	Room	Room
Drapes/curtain/blind/	_____	_____	_____
hardware broken/missing	_____	_____	_____
Window/door not placed/	_____	_____	_____
square/jammed	_____	_____	_____
Hardware broken/missing	_____	_____	_____
Glass broken/uncaulked	_____	_____	_____
Weatherstripping missing	_____	_____	_____
Condensate between panels	_____	_____	_____
Improper swing	_____	_____	_____
_____	_____	_____	_____
_____	_____	_____	_____
_____	_____	_____	_____

Comments: _____

_____

_____

Utilities:

	Room	Room	Room
Electrical receptacle broken/	_____	_____	_____
missing/wired wrong	_____	_____	_____
Circuit unenergized	_____	_____	_____
Light switch broken/	_____	_____	_____
missing/wrong location	_____	_____	_____
Diffusers/air returns/	_____	_____	_____
missing/not flush	_____	_____	_____
Telephone jack/TV cable/	_____	_____	_____
missing/wrong location	_____	_____	_____
Baseboard heater loose	_____	_____	_____
No hot water	_____	_____	_____
No cold water	_____	_____	_____
Security light	_____	_____	_____
Alarm doesn't work	_____	_____	_____
Smoke/heat detectors/	_____	_____	_____
missing or broken	_____	_____	_____
_____	_____	_____	_____
_____	_____	_____	_____

Comments: _____

_____

_____

Main Entrance:

	Yes	No	Notations
Leaking canopy			
Doorbell work			
Peephole installed			
Threshold plate tight			
Outside light work			
Light switch inside door			
Doors tight when latched			
Snow guard on roof			
Coat hooks installed			
_____			
_____			
_____			

Kitchen:

	Yes	No	Notations
Appliances work			
Vent hood exhausts			
Dishwasher temp okay			
Counters level/grouted			
Backsplash in place			
Counter height right			
Cabinets fit well			
Doors and drawers work			
GFCI outlets at sink			
Pass through window intact			
_____			
_____			
_____			

Rear Entrance

	Yes	No	Notations
Overhead okay	_____	_____	_____
Landing level	_____	_____	_____
Doorbell work	_____	_____	_____
Threshold plate tight	_____	_____	_____
Outside light work	_____	_____	_____
Light switch inside door	_____	_____	_____
Doors tight when latched	_____	_____	_____
Snow guard on roof	_____	_____	_____
_____	_____	_____	_____
_____	_____	_____	_____
_____	_____	_____	_____

Living Room:

	Yes	No	Notations
Ceiling fan work	_____	_____	_____
Thermostat work	_____	_____	_____
Fireplace damper functional	_____	_____	_____
Mantel flush against wall	_____	_____	_____
_____	_____	_____	_____
_____	_____	_____	_____
_____	_____	_____	_____
_____	_____	_____	_____
_____	_____	_____	_____
_____	_____	_____	_____
_____	_____	_____	_____
_____	_____	_____	_____
_____	_____	_____	_____
_____	_____	_____	_____
_____	_____	_____	_____
_____	_____	_____	_____
_____	_____	_____	_____

Dining Room:

	Yes	No	Notations
Chandelier hung	_____	_____	_____
Rheostat works	_____	_____	_____
China cupboard finished	_____	_____	_____
Room exhaust works	_____	_____	_____
_____	_____	_____	_____
_____	_____	_____	_____
_____	_____	_____	_____
_____	_____	_____	_____
_____	_____	_____	_____
_____	_____	_____	_____
_____	_____	_____	_____
_____	_____	_____	_____
_____	_____	_____	_____
_____	_____	_____	_____
_____	_____	_____	_____
_____	_____	_____	_____
_____	_____	_____	_____
_____	_____	_____	_____
_____	_____	_____	_____

Utility Room:

	Yes	No	Notations
Washer hook-ups in	_____	_____	_____
Dryer outlet work/vent	_____	_____	_____
Deep sink properly installed	_____	_____	_____
Linen closets okay	_____	_____	_____
Water available at taps	_____	_____	_____
Floor drain drains	_____	_____	_____
Built-in cupboard okay	_____	_____	_____
_____	_____	_____	_____
_____	_____	_____	_____
_____	_____	_____	_____
_____	_____	_____	_____
_____	_____	_____	_____
_____	_____	_____	_____
_____	_____	_____	_____
_____	_____	_____	_____
_____	_____	_____	_____
_____	_____	_____	_____
_____	_____	_____	_____

Master Bedroom and Bath:

	Yes	No	Notations
Closet shelving installed			
Vanity heights right			
GFCI outlets test out			
Fixtures drain slow			
Ceramic tile grout okay			
Countertop level			
Fixtures have stop valves			
Nonskid tub surface			
All accessories built-in			
Mixing valves work			
Any fixtures leak			
Drawers and doors work			
Plumbing access door			

Second Bedroom and Bath:

	Yes	No	Notations
Closet okay			
Vanity right height			
GFCI outlets test out			
Fixtures work without leaks			
Stop valves at fixtures			
Tub/shower work			
Mixing valves work			
Counters level			
Drawers and doors work			
Accessories built-in			
Plumbers access door			
Drains drain slow			
_____			
_____			
_____			
_____			
_____			
_____			
_____			

Third Bedroom and Bath:

	Yes	No	Notations
Closet okay	_____	_____	_____
Vanity right height	_____	_____	_____
GFCI outlets test out	_____	_____	_____
Fixtures work without leaks	_____	_____	_____
Stop valves at fixtures	_____	_____	_____
Tub/shower work	_____	_____	_____
Mixing valves work	_____	_____	_____
Counters level	_____	_____	_____
Drawers and doors work	_____	_____	_____
Accessories built-in	_____	_____	_____
Plumbers access door	_____	_____	_____
Drains drain slow	_____	_____	_____
_____	_____	_____	_____
_____	_____	_____	_____
_____	_____	_____	_____
_____	_____	_____	_____
_____	_____	_____	_____
_____	_____	_____	_____
_____	_____	_____	_____
_____	_____	_____	_____

Garage:

	Yes	No	Notations
Garage doors work	_____	_____	_____
Door to house okay	_____	_____	_____
Outside light works	_____	_____	_____
Concrete floor cracked	_____	_____	_____
Workbench installed	_____	_____	_____
Pegboard up	_____	_____	_____
Crawlspace opening	_____	_____	_____
_____	_____	_____	_____
_____	_____	_____	_____
_____	_____	_____	_____
_____	_____	_____	_____
_____	_____	_____	_____
_____	_____	_____	_____
_____	_____	_____	_____
_____	_____	_____	_____
_____	_____	_____	_____
_____	_____	_____	_____
_____	_____	_____	_____
_____	_____	_____	_____

Basement:

	Yes	No	Notations
Louvre in entry door			
Electric panels covered			
Circuits labeled			
Ductwork insulated			
Pipes wrapped			
Safety valves tested			
Pilot light lit			
Furnace/boiler work			
Water heater work			
Water pressure okay			

Other Rooms:

	Yes	No	Notations

Other Rooms (cont.):

	Yes	No	Notations

Exterior Observation:

Cracks in surfaces _____

Unpainted trim _____

Missing materials _____

Caulking missing _____

Window wells proper _____

Gutters properly installed _____

Vents and chimney capped _____

Drives/walks cracked _____

Shrubbery planted _____

Grass growing _____

Outbuildings completed _____

_____ _____

_____ _____

_____ _____

Notes

_____

_____

_____

_____

_____

_____

_____

_____

_____

_____

_____

_____

_____

_____

_____

_____

_____

INSPECTED BY: _____   DATE _____

SUBMITTED TO: _____   DATE _____

COPIES TO: _____   DATE _____

Appendix A
Glossary

abstract of title A summary of the public records relating to the title to a particular piece of land. An attorney or title insurance company reviews an abstract of title to determine whether there are any title defects that must be cleared before a buyer can purchase clear, marketable, and insurable title.

acceleration clause Condition in a mortgage that might require the balance of the loan to become due immediately, if regular mortgage payments are not made or for breach of other conditions of the mortgage.

adverse possession A statute of limitations that bars the true owner from asserting his claim to the land where he has remained silent and has done nothing to stop the adverse occupant during the statutory period varying from seven to thirty years.

agreement of sale A contract in which a seller agrees to sell and a buyer to buy, under specific terms and conditions spelled out in writing and signed by both parties; known by various names, such as contract of purchase, purchase agreement, or sales agreement according to location or jurisdiction.

American Plywood Association A trade association representing most of the nation's manufacturers of construction plywood. The association has three main jobs: research to improve plywood performance and products; inspection and testing to ensure plywood's consistently high quality; and promotion and information service.

amortization Provision for gradually paying off the principal amount of a loan, such as a mortgage loan, at the time of each payment of interest. For example, as each payment toward principal is made, the mortgage amount is reduced or amortized by that amount.

appraisal   An evaluation of the property to determine its value. An appraisal is concerned chiefly with market value—what the house would sell for in the market place.

as built drawings   Record drawings made during construction. As built drawings record the locations, sizes, and nature of concealed items such as structural elements, accessories, equipment, devices, plumbing lines, valves, mechanical equipment, and the like. These records (with dimensions) form a permanent record for future reference.

assessed value   A percentage of appraised value for tax purposes. It's confusing and meant to be. If it were clear, the common people could understand it. The tax rate is a certain amount for each one hundred dollars of assessed value.

assumption of mortgage   An obligation undertaken by the purchaser of property to be personally liable for payment of an existing mortgage. In an assumption, the purchaser is substituted for the original mortgagor in the mortgage instrument and the original mortgagor is released from further liability under the mortgage. Since the mortgagor is to be released from further liability in the assumption, the mortgagee's consent is usually required.

astragal   A molding attached to one of a pair of double doors against which the other strikes when they are closed.

auger   A tool used to make cylindrical holes in building materials or the earth.

backfill   Earth or earthen material used to fill the excavation around a foundation; the act of filling around a foundation.

bid bond   A bond secured by the bidder from a surety that guarantees that he will enter into a contract within a specified time period subject to forfeiture if the date is not met.

binder or offer to purchase   A preliminary agreement, secured by the payment of earnest money, between a buyer and seller as an offer to purchase real estate. A binder secures the right to purchase real estate upon agreed terms for a limited period of time. If the buyer changes his mind or is unable to purchase, the earnest money is forfeited unless the binder expressly provides that it is to be refunded.

BOCA   Building Officials and Code Administrators International, Inc., an organization that publishes a model building code.

bridge loan   A short-term loan to bridge the time between the purchase of one house and the sale of another.

building codes   The minimum legal requirements established or adopted by a government such as a municipality. Building codes are established by ordinance, and govern the design and construction of buildings.

building line or setback   Distances from the ends and/or sides of the lot beyond which construction cannot extend. The building line can be established by a filed plat of subdivision, by restrictive covenants in deeds or leases, by building codes, or by zoning ordinances.

building permit   A written authorization required by ordinance for a specific project. A building permit allows construction to proceed in accordance with construction documents approved by the building official.

built-up roof (bur) A roof membrane laminated from layers of asphalt-saturated felt or other fabric, bonded together with bitumen or pitch.

casement window A window that swings out to the side on hinges.

cantilever A beam, truss, or slab that extends beyond its last point of support.

certificate of insurance A written document appropriately signed by a responsible representative of the insurance company and stating the exact coverage and period of time for which the coverage is applicable in accordance with requirements of the contract documents.

certificate of title The paper that signifies ownership of a house. It usually contains a legal description of the house and its land.

change order A written document signed by the owner, design professional, and contractor, detailing a change or modification to the contract for construction.

cladding A material used as the exterior wall enclosure of a building.

cleanout Drains blockage in waste or drain lines. A plumbing fitting, "Y," "T," "L," or a coupling should be installed at the end of all waste or drain lines. These fittings should include a screw plug or cap for ease of cleanout under sink and bath lavatory.

closing costs Sometimes called settlement costs, costs in addition to price of house, including mortgage service charges, title search and insurance, and transfer of ownership charges. Be sure your sales contract clearly states who will pay each of these costs—buyer or seller.

collar beam Beam, usually made of wood, used to connect opposite rafters together; sometimes called straining piece.

contingency allowance A specified sum, included in the contract sum. A contingency allowance is intended to be used, at the owner's discretion, and with his approval, to pay for any element or service related to the construction that is desirable to the owner, but not specifically required of the contractor by the construction documents.

contract documents A term applied to any combination of related documents that collectively define the extent of an agreement between two or more parties. As regards to the contract for construction, the contract documents generally consist of the agreement (contract), the bonds, the certificates, the conditions of the contract, the specifications, the drawings, and the modifications.

contractor's qualification statement A statement of the contractor's qualifications, experience, financial condition, business history, and staff composition. This statement, together with listed business and professional references, provides evidence of the contractor's competence to perform the work and assume the responsibilities required by the contract documents.

conventional mortgage A mortgage loan not insured by HUD or guaranteed by the Veterans' Administration. It is subject to conditions established by the lending institution and state statutes. The mortgage rates can vary with different institutions and between states.

damper A flap to control or obstruct the flow of gases; specifically, a metal control flap in the throat of a fireplace, or in an air duct.

deed A formal written instrument by which title to real property is transferred from one owner to another. The deed should contain an accurate description of the property being conveyed, should be signed and witnessed according to the laws of the state where the property is located, and should be delivered to the purchaser at closing day. There are two parties to a deed: the grantor and the grantee.

depreciation Decline in value of a house due to wear and tear, adverse changes in the neighborhood, or any other reason.

dew point The temperature at which water will begin to condense from a mass of air at a given temperature and moisture content.

documentary stamps A state tax, in the form of stamps, required on deeds and mortgages when real estate title passes from one owner to another. The amount of stamps required varies with each state.

downpayment The amount of money to be paid by the purchaser to the seller upon the signing of the agreement of sale. The agreement of sale will refer to the downpayment amount and will acknowledge receipt of the downpayment. Downpayment is the difference between the sales price and the maximum mortgage amount. The downpayment might not be refundable if the purchaser fails to buy the property without good cause. If the purchaser wants the downpayment to be refundable, he should insert a clause in the agreement of sale specifying the conditions under which the deposit will be refunded, if the agreement does not already contain such clause. If the seller cannot deliver good title, the agreement of sale usually requires the seller to return the downpayment and to pay interest and expenses incurred by the purchaser.

drawn glass Glass sheet pulled directly from a container of molten glass.

dwv Drain-waste-vent pipes, the part of the plumbing system of a building that removes liquid wastes and conducts them to the sewer or sewage disposal system.

earnest money The deposit given to the seller by the potential buyer to show that he is serious about buying the house. If the deal goes through, the earnest money is applied against the downpayment. If the deal does not go through it can be forfeited.

easement rights A right-of-way granted to a person or company authorizing access to or over the owner's land. An electric company obtaining a right-of-way across private property is a common example.

efflorescence A powdery deposit on the face of a structure of masonry or concrete, caused by the leaching of chemical salts by water migrating from within the structure to the surface.

eminent domain Taking of land by government for public use.

encroachment An obstruction, building, or part of a building that intrudes beyond a legal boundary onto neighboring private or public land, or a building extending beyond the building line.

encumbrance A legal right or interest in land that affects a good or clear title, and diminishes the land's value. It can take numerous forms, such as zoning ordinances, easement rights, claims, mortgages, liens, charges, a pending legal action, unpaid taxes, or restrictive covenants. An encumbrance does not legally prevent transfer of the property to another. A title search is all that is usually done to reveal the existence of such encumbrances, and it is up to the buyer to determine whether he wants to purchase with the encumbrance, or what can be done to remove it.

endorsement A document, supplemental to an insurance policy covering a specified loss; an endorsement modifies the conditions of the contract terms stated on the face of the insurance policy.

engineered fill Earth compacted into place in such a way that it has predictable physical properties, based on laboratory tests and specified, supervised installation procedures.

equity The value of a homeowner's unencumbered interest in real estate. Equity is computed by subtracting from the property's fair market value the total of the unpaid mortgage balance and any outstanding liens or other debts against the property. A homeowner's equity increases as he pays off his mortgage or as the property appreciates in value. When the mortgage and all other debts against the property are paid in full the homeowner has 100% equity in his property.

escheat Death of an owner leaving no heir or legal claimant; his property reverts to the state under the doctrine of escheat.

escrow Funds paid by one party to another (the escrow agent) to hold until the occurrence of a specified event, after which the funds are released to a designated individual. In FHA mortgage transactions an escrow account usually refers to the funds a mortgagor pays the lender at the time of the periodic mortgage payments. The money is held in a trust fund, provided by the lender for the buyer. Such funds should be adequate to cover yearly anticipated expenditures for mortgage insurance premiums, taxes, hazard insurance premiums, and special assessments.

expansion joint A discontinuity extending completely through the foundation, frame, and finishes of a building to allow for gross movement due to thermal stress, material separation or settlement of the foundation.

FHA loan A loan in which the Federal Housing Administration, a branch of the federal government, insures your mortgage to the lending bank. FHA has nationwide minimum property standards, or building code, which must be met. This book attempts to meet these codes in every way possible.

field order A written modification to the contract for construction, made by the design professional, the construction administrator, or the construction manager. A field order documents a change to the contract documents in anticipation of the issuance of a formal change order signed by owner, design professional, and contractor.

fire separation wall A wall required under the building code to divide two parts of a building as a deterrent to the spread of fire.

firestop A wood or masonry baffle used to close an opening between studs or joists in a balloon or platform frame in order to retard the spread of fire through the opening.

fire wall A wall extending from foundation to roof, required under the building code to divide two parts of a building as a deterrent to the spread of fire.

flashing Galvanized sheet metal used as a lining around joints between shingles and chimneys, exhaust and ventilation vents, and other protrusions in the roof deck. Flashing helps prevent water from seeping under the shingles.

foreclosure A legal term applied to any of the various methods of enforcing payment of the debt secured by a mortgage or deed of trust, by taking and selling the mortgaged property, and depriving the mortgagor of possession.

formwork Temporary structures of wood, steel, or plastic that serve to give shape to poured concrete and to support it and keep it moist as it cures.

framing plan A diagram showing the arrangement and sizes of the structural members in a floor or roof.

gambrel A roof shape consisting of two roof planes at different pitches on each side of a ridge.

general warranty deed A deed that conveys not only all the grantor's interests in and title to the property to the grantee, but also warrants that if the title is defective or

has a "cloud" on it (such as mortgage claims, tax liens, title claims, judgments, or mechanic's liens against it) the grantee can hold the grantor liable.

girder A wood beam built up of three 2 × 8s bolted together, or a 6-inch I beam running the full length of the home, installed under a wood floor for a crawl-space or basement home. This girder carries the weight of the floor and walls, and a portion of the roof weight. For crawl-space home, the girder is mounted on concrete piers and blocks. For basement homes, the girder is supported by adjustable jack posts.

grantee That party in the deed who is the buyer or recipient.

grantor That party in the deed who is the seller or giver.

ground fault interrupter A safety device that monitors the difference between current flowing through the hot and neutral wire. If there is an imbalance of current greater than five milliamps, the current will be cut off instantly. The GFI measures for electric current leakage.

hazard insurance Insurance to protect against damages caused to property by fire, windstorm, and other common hazards.

home mortgage loan A special kind of long-term loan for buying a house. There are three kinds of mortgage financing for single-family homes in the United States—the conventional mortgage; the VA (Veterans Administration), sometimes called the GI mortgage; and the HUD-insured loan.

hose bibb An outside water faucet for connecting a lawn hose. In a cold climate, a special faucet is needed to avoid freezing in winter. The average home should have at least two outside faucets.

hose test A standard laboratory test to determine the relative ability of an interior building assembly to stand up to water from a firehose during a fire.

HUD United States Department of Housing and Urban Development. Office of Housing/Federal Housing Administration within HUD insures home mortgage loans made by lenders and sets minimum standards for such homes.

hydronic heating system A system that circulates warm water through convectors to heat a building.

insulating board A low-density board made of wood, sugarcane, cornstalks, or similar materials, usually formed by a felting process, dried and usually pressed to thicknesses of $1/2$ and $5/32$ inches.

interceptor drain A ditch cut into a hillside on an angle to collect water and direct it away from your house.

interim financing A short-term loan. It is generally converted to a long-term loan at a later date.

invitation to bid A written notice of an owner's intention to receive competitive bids for a construction project wherein a select group of candidate constructors are invited to submit proposals.

involuntary alienation Transfer of property without owners consent such as tax sale, judgment liens, or bankruptcy.

involute Curved portion of trim used to terminate a piece of staircase railing; normally used on traditional homes.

jack rafter A shortened rafter that joins a hip or valley rafter.

joist One of a series of parallel beams used to support floor and ceiling loads, and supported in turn by larger beams, girders, or bearing walls.

journeyman The second or intermediate level of development of proficiency in a particular trade or skill. As related to building construction, a journeyman's license, earned by a combination of education, supervised experience and examination, is required in many areas for those employed as intermediate level mechanics in certain trades (e.g., plumbing, mechanical, and electrical work).

judgment A judicial decision rendered as a result of a course of action in a court of law.

kerf The area of a board removed by the saw when cutting; a slot.

key A slot formed into a concrete surface for the purpose of interlocking with a subsequent pour of concrete, a slot at the edge of a precast member into which grout will be poured to lock it to an adjacent member.

laminated beam A very strong beam created from several smaller pieces of wood that have been glued together under heat and pressure.

ledger strip A strip of lumber nailed along the bottom of the side of a girder on which joists rest.

let-in bracing Diagonal bracing nailed into notches cut in the face on the studs so it does not increase the thickness of the wall.

lien A claim by one person on the property of another as security for money owed. Such claims may include obligations not met or satisfied, judgments, unpaid taxes, materials, or labor.

life cycle A term often used to

describe the period of time that a building can be expected to actively and adequately serve its intended function.

litigation Legal action or process in a court of law.

low-emissivity coating A surface coating for glass that permits the passage of most shortwave electromagnetic radiation (light and heat), but reflects most long-wave radiation (heat).

marketable title A title that is free and clear of objectional liens, clouds, or other title defects. A title that enables an owner to sell his property freely to others and which others will accept without objection.

mechanic's lien A type of lien filed by one who has performed work related to the real property for which compensation is either in dispute or remains unsatisfied.

medium-range sealant A sealant material that is capable of a moderate degree of elongation before rupture.

modulus of elasticity An index of the stiffness of a material, derived by measuring the elastic deformation of the material as it is placed under stress, and then dividing the stress by the deformation.

moment A twisting action; a torque; a force acting at a distance from a point in a structure so as to cause a tendency of the structure to rotate about that point.

mortgage A lien or claim against real property given by the buyer to the lender as security for money borrowed. Under government-insured or loan-guarantee provisions, the payments can include escrow amounts covering taxes, hazard insurance, water charges, and special assessments. Mortgages generally run from 10 to 30 years, during which the loan is to be paid off.

mortgage commitment The written notice from the bank or other lender saying that it will advance you the mortgage funds in a specified amount to enable you to buy the house.

mortgagee The bank or lender who loans the money to the mortgagor.

mortgage note A written agreement to repay a loan. The agreement is secured by a mortgage, serves as proof of an indebtedness, and states the manner in which it shall be paid. The note states the actual amount of the debt that the mortgage secures and renders the mortgagor personally responsible for repayment.

mortgagor The homeowner who is obligated to repay a mortgage loan on a property he has purchased.

nail popping The loosening of nails holding gypsum board to a wall, caused by drying shrinkage of the studs.

needle beam A steel or wood beam threaded through a hole in a bearing wall and used to support the wall and its superimposed loads during underpinning of its foundation.

newel The upright post or the upright formed by the inner or smaller ends of steps about which steps of a circular staircase wind. In a straight flight staircase, the principal post at the foot or the secondary post at a landing.

nominal dimension An approximate dimension assigned to a piece of material as a convenience in referring to the piece.

obligated room A room that you have to go through to get to another room.

Occupational Safety and Health Act (OSHA) Act sometimes referred to as the Williams-Steiger Act. Enacted by Congress in 1970, it was designed to improve job safety under administration of the U.S. Department of Labor, with provision of fines and penalties for noncompliance.

performance specification A description of the desired results of performance of a product, material, assembly, or piece of equipment with criteria for verifying compliance.

perimeter foundation The outside wall of the house; this is what the house rests on.

pitch The incline or rise of a roof. Pitch is expressed in inches or rise per root of run, or by the ratio of the rise to the span.

plat A map or chart of a lot, subdivision or community drawn by a surveyor showing boundary lines, buildings, improvements on the land, and easements.

plenum A chamber that can serve as a distribution area for heating or cooling systems, generally between a false ceiling and the actual ceiling.

points One percent of the amount of the mortgage loan; sometimes called "discount points." For example, if a loan is for $25,000, one point is $250. Points are charged by a lender to raise the yield on his loan at a time when money is tight, interest rates are high, and there is a legal limit to the interest rate that can be charged on a mortgage. Buyers are prohibited from paying points on HUD or Veterans' Administration guaranteed loans (sellers can pay, however). On a conventional mortgage, points may be paid by either buyer or seller or split between them.

prepaid expenses The initial deposit at time of closing, for taxes and hazard insurance and the subsequent monthly deposits made to the lender for that purpose.

principal The basic element of the loan as distinguished from interest and mortgage insurance premium. In other words, principal is the amount upon which interest is paid.

promissory note A legal instrument, agreement, or contract made between a lender and a borrower by which the lender conveys to the borrower a sum or other consideration known as principal for which the borrower promises repayment of the principal plus interest under conditions set forth in the agreement.

proprietary specification A type of specification that describes a product, material, assembly, or piece of equipment by trade name and/or by naming the manufacturer or manufacturers who might produce products acceptable to the owner or design professional.

punch list A list of items within a project, prepared by the contractor, confirmed by the owner or his representative that can remain to be replaced or completed in accordance with the requirements of the contract for construction at the time of substantial completion.

purchase order A written contract or similar agreement made between a buyer and seller that details the items to be purchased, the price of such items, and the method and responsibility for delivery and acceptance of the items. A purchase order also formalizes the intentions of both parties to the transaction.

quarry An excavation from which building stone is obtained; the act of taking stone from the ground.

quitclaim deed A deed that transfers whatever interest the maker of the deed might have in the particular parcel of land. A quitclaim deed is often given to clear the title when the grantor's interest in a property is questionable. By accepting such a deed the buyer assumes all the risks. Such a deed makes no warranties as to the title, but simply transfers to the buyer whatever interest the grantor has.

quoin Fancy edging on outside covers made of brick veneer or stucco.

radiant heat Coils of electricity, hot water, or steam pipes embedded in floors, ceilings, or walls to heat rooms.

real estate broker A middle man or agent who buys and sells real estate for a company, firm, or individual on a commission basis. The broker does not have title to the property, but generally represents the owner.

real property Land and all things firmly attached to it above ground or contained within the earth below ground.

recording fee The fee charged to record legal documents in place of permanent records, such as a county courthouse.

refinancing The process of the same mortgagor paying off one loan with the proceeds from another loan.

reflective coated glass Glass onto which a thin layer of metal or metal oxide has been deposited to reflect light and/or heat.

reinforced concrete Concrete strengthened with wire, metal bars, or fiberglass bars or particles.

restrictive covenants Private restrictions limiting the use of real property. Restrictive covenants are created by deed and can *run with the land*, binding all subsequent purchasers of the land, or can be *personal* and binding only between the original seller and buyer. The determination whether a covenant runs with the land or is personal is governed by the language of the covenant, the intent of the parties, and the law in the state where the land is situated. Restrictive covenants that run with the land are encumbrances and can effect the value and marketability of title. Restrictive covenants can limit the density of buildings per acre, regulate size, style, or price range of buildings to be erected, or prevent particular businesses from operating or minority groups from owning or occupying homes in a given area. (This latter discriminatory covenant is unconstitutional and has been declared unenforcible by the U.S. Supreme Court.)

ridge Intersection of any two roofing planes where water drains away from the intersection. Special shingles are applied to ridges.

sash The movable part of the window; the frame in which panes of glass are set in a window or door.

second mortgage The pledging of property to a lender as security for repayment, but using property that has already been pledged for a loan.

sedimentary rock Rock formed from materials deposited as sediments, such as sand or sea shells, which form sandstone and limestone, respectively.

selective bidding A process of competitive bidding for award of the contract for construction whereby the owner selects the constructors who are invited to bid to the exclusion of others as in the process of open bidding.

septic tank A sewage settling tank in which part of the sewage is converted into gas and sludge before the remaining waste is discharged by gravity into a leaching bed underground.

setback line In most areas, your home must be a certain distance back from the street and from your side-yard property lines. You must determine your local restrictions before building.

settling Movement of unstable dirt over time. Fill dirt normally settles downward as it is compacted by its own weight or a structure above it.

shop drawings Detailed plans prepared by a fabricator to guide the shop production of such building components as cut stonework, steel, or precast concrete framing, curtain wall panels, and cabinetwork.

smoke developed rating An index of the toxic fumes generated by a material as it burns.

Sound Transmission Class (STC) An index of the resistance of a partition to the passage of sound.

special assessments A special tax imposed on property, individual lots or all property in the immediate area, for road construction, sidewalks, sewers, street lights, etc.

special lien A lien that binds a specified piece of property, unlike a general lien, which is levied against all one's assets. It creates a right to retain something of value belonging to another person as compensation for labor, material, or money expended in that person's behalf. In some localities it is called *particular* lien or *specific* lien.

special warranty deed A deed in which the grantor conveys title to the grantee and agrees to protect the grantee against title defects or claims asserted by the grantor and those persons whose right to assert a claim against the title arose during the period the grantor held title to the property. In a special warranty deed the grantor guarantees to the grantee that he has done nothing during the time he held title to the property that has, or that might in the future, impair the grantee's title.

specifications The written instructions from an architect or engineer concerning the quality of materials and workmanship required for a building.

squatters' rights People who settle on land without a claim—if permitted for more than the statutory period. They could obtain an easement by prescription.

statutes of limitation Provision of law establishing a certain time limit from an occurrence during which a judgment can be sought from a court of law.

statutory requirements Requirements that are embodied in the law.

subcontractor A contractor who specializes in one area of construction activity, and who usually works under a general contractor.

subfloor Usually, plywood sheets that are nailed directly to the floor joists and receive the finish flooring.

substantial completion The condition when the work of the project is substantially complete, ready for the owner's acceptance and occupancy. Any items remaining to be completed should, at this point, be duly noted or stipulated in writing.

summer switch A switch on a forced-air furnace to operate the fan manually with no heat; a good idea on a hot day.

surety An individual or company that provides a bond or pledge to guarantee that another individual or company will perform in accordance with the terms of an agreement or contract.

survey A map or plat made by a licensed surveyor showing the results of measuring the land with its elevations, improvements, boundaries, and its relationship to surrounding tracts of land. A survey is often required by the lender to assure him that a building is actually sited on the land according to its legal descriptions.

tail beam A relatively short beam or joist supported in a wall on one end and by a header on the other.

take-off The compilation of a list of materials used for a particular phase of construction, such as the number of bricks or the number and sizes of windows; also called a schedule of materials.

tax stamp A stamp affixed to a legal document to indicate that a tax has been paid.

tenants by the entirety A joint title shared by husband and wife. This is secure against law suits in that the property cannot be forcibly sold to satisfy a judgment against one of you.

tenants in common Joint possession of the property by both tenants, but each has separate interests and distinct titles. Each tenant can separately sell his interest.

title The rights of ownership and possession of a particular property. In real estate usage, title can refer to the instruments or documents by which a right of ownership is established (title documents), or it can refer to the ownership interest one has in the real estate.

title insurance Insurance that protects lenders or homeowners against loss of their interest in property due to legal defects in title. Title insurance can be issued to either the mortgagor, as an owner's title policy, or to the mortgagee, as a mortgagee's title policy. Insurance benefits will be paid only to the *named insured* in the title policy, so it is important that an owner purchase an *owner's title policy*, if he desires the protection of title insurance.

title search or examination A check of the title records, generally at the local courthouse, to make sure the buyer is purchasing a house from the legal owner, and there are no liens, overdue special assessments, or other claims or outstanding restrictive covenants filed in the record, which would adversely affect the marketability or value of title.

transit A surveying instrument used to measure horizontal angles, levelness, and vertical depth.

truss A combination of structural members usually arranged in triangular units to form a rigid framework for spanning between load-bearing walls.

trustee A party who is given legal responsibility to hold property in the best interest of or for the benefit of another. The trustee is one placed in a position of responsibility for another, a responsibility enforceable in a court of law.

turn key A contract that provides all of the services required to produce a building or other construction project.

undercarpet wiring system Flat, insulated electrical conductors that are run under carpeting, and their associated outlet boxes and fixtures.

underlayment Any paper or felt composition used to separate the roofing deck from the shingles.

unit cost contract A contract for construction where compensation is based on a stipulated cost per unit of measure for the volume of work produced.

unsecured loan A loan in which no material possessions are pledged as security for repayment.

vapor barrier Material such as paper, metal, or paint that is used to prevent vapor from passing from rooms into the outside walls.

vent pipe A pipe that allows gas to escape from plumbing systems.

vermiculite Expanded mica, used as an insulating fill or a lightweight aggregate.

wainscoting The lower three or four feet of an interior wall when lined with paneling, tile, or other material different from the rest of the wall.

warranty Manufacturer's certification of quality and performance that can include a limited guarantee of satisfaction.

water-resistant gypsum board A gypsum board designed for use in wet locations.

water table The level at which the pressure of water in the soil is equal to atmospheric pressure; effectively, the level to which ground water will fill an excavation.

wattage Value of electrical power; the product of the amperage times the voltage; the amount of electrical power needed to run a particular appliance.

window well One of these is used on a crawl-space home. This unit reduces the height from the finish wood floor down to the finish grade, giving the home a more pleasant appearance from the street. It allows the basement window to be recessed below grade, out of sight, yet supplies light and ventilation to the basement.

yield strength The stress at which a material ceases to deform in a fully elastic manner.

zoning ordinances The acts of an authorized local government establishing building codes, and setting forth regulations for property land usage.

Appendix B
Sources

ABCA
American Building Contractors Association
8727 W. Third Street
Suite 203
Los Angeles, CA 90048

General, specialty contractors, and subcontractors; lending institutions; utility suppliers, and manufacturers concerned with the building industry; 700 members.

ACCA
Air Conditioning Contractors of America
1228 17th Street, N.W.
Washington, DC 20036

Contractors involved in the installation and servicing of heating, refrigeration, and air conditioning systems; (maintains small library on load calculation and systems design); 2,000 members.

AHAM
Association of Home Appliance Managers
20 N. Wacker
Chicago, IL 60606

Comprised of companies manufacturing approximately 90% of the major appliances and portable appliances in the U.S. each year; does market research and reporting of industry statistics; and development of standards for measuring appliance performance and certification of appliances; 132 members.

AI
Asphalt Institute
Asphalt Institute Bldg.
College Park, MD 20740

Refiners of asphalt products from crude petroleum; conducts extensive program of education, research, and engineering service related to asphaltic products; publishes specifications, engineering manuals, booklets, and other material on asphalt construction; 53 members.

ASC
Adhesive and Sealant Council
1600 Wilson Boulevard
Suite 910
Arlington, VA 22209

Firms manufacturing and selling all rubber and plastic-based adhesives and related sealants in either solid or liquid form; 140 members.

ASHI
American Society of Home Inspectors
1629 K Street, N.W.
Suite 520
Washington, DC 20056

Professional home inspectors, architects, engineers, construction supervisors, and building technicians whose purposes are to establish home inspector qualifications; set standards of practice for home inspections; adhere to a code of ethics, and inform members of the most advanced methods and techniques; 300 members.

BHMA
Builders Hardware Manufacturers Association
60 E. 42nd Street
Room 1807
New York, NY 10165

Manufacturers of builders' hardware both contract and stock; provides statistical services; maintains standardization program; and conducts seminars and conferences; 75 members.

NAHB
National Association of Home Builders of the U.S.
15th and M Streets, N.W.
Washington, DC 20005

Single and multifamily home builders and others associated with the building industry; collects and publishes data on current developments in home building and home builders' plans; sponsors national seminars and workshops on construction, mortgage credit, labor relations, cost reduction, land use, remodeling, and business management; 108,000 members.

NAR
National Association of Realtors
430 N. Michigan Avenue
Chicago, IL 60601

Promotes education, high professional standards, and modern techniques in specialized real estate work such as brokerage, appraisal, property management, and land development; and sponsors a program of realtor involvement in service projects in their communities; 607,000 members.

NEMA
National Electrical Manufacturers Association
2101 L Street N.W.
Washington, DC 20037

Maintains and improves quality and reliability in products; ensures safety standards in manufacture and use of products; and develops product standards covering such matters as nomenclature, ratings, performance, testing, and dimensions of electrical devices; 550 members.

NEREA
National Association of Real Estate Appraisers
853 Broadway
New York, NY 10003

Makes available the services of the most highly qualified real estate appraisers; 1,000 members.

NWMA
National Woodwork Manufacturers Association
205 W. Touhy Avenue
Park Avenue, IL 60068

Manufacturers of woodwork products such as doors, windows, frames, and related products; establishes standards; and conducts research in all areas of door and window manufacture; 110 members.

PCA
Portland Cement Association
5420 Old Orchard Road
Skokie, IL 60077

Manufacturers of portland cement in US and Canada; conducts research on concrete technology and durability, concrete pavement design, load-bearing capacities, field performance and fire resistance of concrete, transportation, building, and structural uses of concrete; 40 members.

UL
Underwriters Laboratory
333 Pfingsten Road
Northbrook, IL 60062

A testing laboratory that investigates, studies, experiments and tests to determine the relation of various materials, devices, products, equipment, construction, methods, and systems to hazards; 2,500 members.

BOOKS

Ahuja, H. N. *Project Management*. New York: John Wiley & Sons, Inc.

Allen, Edward. *Fundamentals of Building Construction*. New York: John Wiley & Sons, Inc.

Bonny, John Bruce. *Handbook of Construction Management and Organization*. New York: Von Nostrand Reinhold Company.

Braugham, Suzanne. *Housewise*. New York: Harper & Row Publishers.

Browne, Don. *The Housebuilding Book*. New York: McGraw-Hill Book Company.

Burch, Monte. *Building Small Barns, Sheds, and Buildings*. Powval, Vermont: Storey Communications, Inc.

Bureau of Naval Personnel. *Basic Construction Techniques For Houses And Small Buildings (simply explained)*. New York: Dover Publications, Inc.

Ching, Francis D.K. *Building Construction Illustrated*. New York: Von Nostrand Reinhold Company, Inc.

Daniel, Alfred H. *The Home Inspection Manual*. Powval, Vermont: Storey Communications, Inc.

de Benedictis, Daniel J. *The Complete Real Estate Adviser*. New York: Pocket Books.

De Cristoforo, R.J. *Housebuilding: A Do It Yourself Guide*. New York: Sterling Publishing Co., Inc.

Falcone, Joseph D. *How to Design, Build, Remodel & Maintain Your Home.* New York: John Wiley & Sons, Inc.

Heldmann, Carl. *Be Your Own House Contractor.* Powval, Vermont: Storey Communications, Inc.

Hoffman, George Cleborn. *How to Inspect A House.* Reading, Massachusetts: Addison-Wesley Publishing Company.

O'Brien, James Jerome. *Construction Inspection Handbook.* New York: Von Nostrand Reinhold Company, Inc.

Phelps, John. *Complete Building Construction.* Indianapolis: The Bobbs-Merrill Co., Inc.

Roskind, Robert. *Building Your Own House.* Berkeley, California: 10 Speed Press.

Taunton Publications. *Tips And Techniques For Builders.* Newtown, Connecticut: The Taunton Press, Inc.

Teets, Robert L. *Profitable Management For The Subcontractor.* New York: McGraw-Hill Book Company.

Training Publications Division of the Bureau of Naval Personnel. *Tools and Their Uses.* New York: Bonanza Books.

PERIODICALS

Construction Specifier
601 Madison Street
Alexandria, VA 22314
(Monthly)

Draperies and Window Coverings
L.C. Clark Publishing Co.
Box 13029
North Palm Beach, FL 33408
(Monthly)

Electrical Apparatus
Borks Publications, Inc.
400 N. Michigan Avenue
Chicago, IL 60611-4198
(Monthly)

Fine Homebuilding
The Taunton Press, Inc.
63 S. Main Street
Box 355
Newtown, CT 06470
(Bimonthly)

Flooring Magazine
7500 Old Oak Blvd.
Cleveland, OH 44130
(Monthly)

Hardware Age
Chilton Company
Chilton Way
Radnor, PA 19089
(Monthly)

Hardware Merchandiser
The Irving-Cloud Publishing Company
7300 N. Cicero
Lincolnwood, IL 60646
(Monthly)

Home, Creative Ideas for Home Design
Knapp Publishing Corp.
Box 92000
Los Angeles, CA 90009
(Monthly)

Home Furnishings
Box 581207
Dallas, TX 75258
(Quarterly)

Home Lighting and Accessories
Box 2147
Clifton, NJ 07015
(Monthly)

Homeowner
Family Media, Inc.
3 Park Avenue
New York, NY 10016
(Monthly)

Journal of Property Management
Institute of Real Estate Management
430 N. Michigan Avenue
Chicago, IL 60611
(Bimonthly)

New Home, The Magazine for Imaginative Homeowners
Gilford Publishing
Box 2008, Village West
Laconia, NH 03246
(Bimonthly)

Practical Homeowner
Rodale Press
33 E. Minor Street
Emmanus, PA 18098
(9 times/year)

Remodeling
Hanley-Wood, Inc.
Suite 475
655 15th Street N.W.
Washington, DC 20005
(Monthly)

Roofing/Siding/Insulation
Harcourt Brace Jovanovich Publications, Inc.
7500 Old Oak Blvd.
Cleveland, OH 44130
(Monthly)

Tile World
Tradeline Publishing Company
485 Kinderkanock Road
Oradell, NJ 07649
(Quarterly)

Walls & Ceilings
8602 N. 40th Street
Tampa, FL 33604
(Monthly)

Appendix C
Handy Reference Tables

Table 1. Appliance Energy Requirements

Major Appliances	Annual KWH
Air-conditioner (room) (Based on 1000 hours of operation per year. This figure will vary widely depending on geographic area and specific size of unit.)	860
Clothes Dryer	993
Dishwasher (including energy used to heat water)	2,100
Dishwasher only	363
Freezer (16 cu. ft.)	1,190
Freezer - frostless (16.5 cu. ft.)	1,820
Range with oven	700
with self-cleaning oven	730
Refrigerator (12 cu. ft.)	728
Refrigerator - frostless (12 cu. ft.)	1,217
Refrigerator/Freezer (12.5 cu. ft.)	1,500
Refrigerator/Freezer - frostless (17.5 cu. ft.)	2,250
Washing Machine - automatic (including energy used to heat water)	2,500
Washing Machine - non-automatic (including energy to heat water)	2,497
washing machine only	76
Water Heater	4,811

Kitchen Appliances

	Annual KWH
Blender	15
Broiler	100
Carving Knife	8
Coffee Maker	140
Deep Fryer	83
Egg Cooker	14
Frying Pan	186
Hot Plate	90
Mixer	13
Oven, Microwave (only)	190
Roaster	205
Sandwich Grill	33
Toaster	39
Trash Compactor	50
Waffle Iron	22
Waste Disposer	30

Heating and Cooling

	Annual KWH
Air Cleaner	216
Electric Blanket	147
Dehumidifier	377
Fan (attic)	281
Fan (circulating)	43
Fan (rollaway)	138
Fan (window)	170
Heater (portable)	176
Humidifier	163

Health and Beauty

Germicidal Lamp	141
Hair Dryer	14
Heat Lamp (infrared)	13
Shaver	1.8
Sun Lamp	16
Toothbrush	.5

Home Entertainment

Radio	86
Television	
Black and White	
Tube type	350
Solid State	120
Color	
Tube type	660
Solid State	440

Housewares

Clock	17
Floor Polisher	15
Sewing Machine	11
Vacuum Cleaner	46

Table 2. Building Design Loads

Occupancy or Use	Live Load Lbs. per Sq. Ft.
Apartment houses:	
Private apartments	40
Public stairways	100
Assembly halls:	
Fixed seats	60
Movable seats	100
Corridors:	
First Floor	100
(Other floors, same as occupancy served	
except as indicated.)	
Dining rooms	100
Dwellings	40
Loft buildings	125
Sidewalks	250
Stairways	100

Table 3. Concrete Curing Methods

Method	Advantage	Disadvantage
Wetting	Excellent results if constantly kept wet	Difficult on vertical walls
Straw	Insulator in winter	Can dry out, blow away or burn
Curing Compounds	Easy to apply Inexpensive	Sprayer needed Can't allow concrete to get too hot
Waterproof Paper	Prevents drying	Cost can be excessive
Plastic Film	Absolutely watertight	Must be weighed down

Table 4. Concrete for Walls
(Per 100 Square Feet Wall)

Thickness	Cubic Feet Required	Cubic Yards Required
4″	33.3	1.24
6″	50.0	1.85
8″	66.7	2.47
10″	83.3	3.09
12″	100.0	3.70

Table 5. Earth Excavation Factors

Depth	Cubic Yards per Square Foot	Depth	Cubic Yards per Square Foot
2″	.006	4′- 6″	.167
4″	.012	5′- 0″	.185
6″	.018	5′- 6″	.204
8″	.025	6′- 0″	.222
10″	.031	6′- 6″	.241
1′- 0″	.037	7′- 0″	.259
1′- 6″	.056	7′- 6″	.278
2′- 0″	.074	8′- 0″	.296
2′- 6″	.093	8′- 6″	.314
3′- 0″	.111	9′- 0″	.332
3′- 6″	.130	9′- 6″	.350
4′- 0″	.148	10′- 0″	.369

Table 6. Geometric Formulas

Circumference of a circle	$C = \pi d$
Length of an arc	$L = \dfrac{n}{360} \times \pi d$
Area of a rectangle	$A = LW$
Area of a square	$A = s^2$
Area of a triangle	$A = \frac{1}{2}bh$
Area of a trapezoid	$A = \frac{1}{2}h\,(b + b')$
Area of a circle	$A = .7854d^2$, or $\frac{1}{4}\pi d^2$
Area of a sector	$S = \dfrac{n}{360} \times .7854d^2$
Area of an ellipse	$A = .7854ab$
Area of the surface of a rectangular solid	$S = 2LW + 2LH + 2WH$
Lateral area of a cylinder	$S = \pi dh$
Area of the surface of a sphere	$S = \pi d^2$
Volume of a rectangular solid	$V = LWH$
Volume of a cylinder	$V = .7854d^2h$
Volume of a sphere	$V = .5236d^3$, or $1/6\pi d^3$
Volume of a cube	$V = e^3$

Table 7. Heat Generated by Appliances

General lights and heating	3.4 BTU/hr/watt
2650 watt toaster	9100 BTU/hr
5000 watt toaster	19,000 BTU/hr
Hair dryer	2000 BTU/hr
Motor less than 2 HP	3600 BTU/hr/HP
Motor over 3 HP	3000 BTU/hr/HP

Table 8. Heat Loss from Hot Water Piping

Pipe Size Inches	Hot Water, 180°F Bare	Insulated
$1/2$	65	22
$3/4$	75	25
1	95	28
$1^1/4$	115	33
$1^1/2$	130	36
2	160	42
$2^1/2$	185	48
3	220	53
4	280	68

Table 9. Length and Area

---

1 statute mile (mi)	= 5280 feet
	= 1.609 kilometers
1 foot (ft)	= 12 inches
	= 30.48 centimeters
1 inch (in)	= 25.40 millimeters
100 ft per min	= 0.508 meter per sec
1 square foot	= 144 sq inches
	= 0.0929 sq meter
1 square inch	= 6.45 sq centimeters
1 kilometer (km)	= 1000 meters
	= 0.621 statute mile
1 meter (m)	= 100 centimeters (cm)
	= 1000 millimeters (m)
	= 1.094 yards
	= 3.281 feet
	= 39.37 inches
1 micron	= 0.001 millimeter
	= 0.000039 inch
1 meter per sec	= 196.9 ft per min

Table 10. Lumber Sizes in Inches

Nominal	Seasoned
1 × 4	$3/4 \times 3^1/_2$
1 × 6	$3/4 \times 5^1/_2$
1 × 8	$3/4 \times 7^1/_4$
1 × 10	$3/4 \times 9^1/_4$
1 × 12	$3/4 \times 11^1/_4$
2 × 4	$1^1/_2 \times 3^1/_2$
2 × 6	$1^1/_2 \times 5^1/_2$
2 × 8	$1^1/_2 \times 7^1/_4$
2 × 10	$1^1/_2 \times 9^1/_4$
2 × 12	$1^1/_2 \times 11^1/_4$
4 × 4	$3^1/_2 \times 3^1/_2$
4 × 6	$3^1/_2 \times 5^1/_2$
4 × 8	$3^1/_2 \times 7^1/_4$
4 × 10	$3^1/_2 \times 9^1/_4$
4 × 12	$3^1/_2 \times 11^1/_4$

Table 11. Miscellaneous Measures

ANGLES OR ARCS

60 seconds (″) .... = 1 minute
60 minutes (′) .... = 1 degree
90 degrees (°) .... = 1 right angle or quadrant
360 degrees .... = 1 circle

AVOIRDUPOIS WEIGHT

437.5 grains (gr.)............................ = 1 ounce
16 ounces (7,000 grains) .... = 1 pound
2,000 pounds................................ = 1 short ton
2,240 pounds................................ = 1 long ton

CUBIC MEASURE

2.728 cubic inches (cu. in.)................... = 1 cubic foot
27 cubic feet................................ = 1 cubic yard

SQUARE MEASURE

144 square inches (sq. in.) .... = 1 square foot
9 square feet .... = 1 square yard

Table 12. Recommended Lighting Levels

AREA	FOOT-CANDLES
Perimeter of building	5
Office areas	70
Corridors, and stairways	20
Toilets and washrooms	30
Entrance lobbies	10
Dining areas	20
Mechanical rooms	20

Table 13. Supply Line Sizes for Common Fixtures

Laundry Tubs................................. = $1/2$ inch
Drinking Fountains .... = $3/8$ inch
Showers..................................... = $1/2$ inch
Water-Closet Tanks .... = $3/8$ inch
Water-Closet (with flush valves)................. = 1 inch
Kitchen Sinks................................. = $1/2$ inch

Table 14. United States Power Characteristics

	VOLTAGE	AMPERES	PHASE
Controls	20 – 120	5 - 15	Single
Small	120		
Equipment	208		
	240	10 – 40	Single
	277		
Large	208		
Equipment	240	30 – 400	Three
	480		

Table 15. Water Requirements of Common Fixtures

FIXTURE	COLD, GPM	HOT, GPM
Water-closet flush valve	45	0
Water-closet flush tank	10	0
Urinals, flush valve	30	0
Urinals, flush tank	10	0
Lavatories	3	3
Shower, 4-in. head	3	3
Shower, 6-in. head and larger	6	6
Baths, tub	5	5
Kitchen sink	4	4
Pantry sink	2	2
Slop Sinks	6	6

Appendix D
Approximate
Construction Costs
(based on 1988 figures)

ITEM	UNIT	COST
ENGINEERING		
Labor		
— principal	hour	85.00
— registered	hour	70.00
— jobsite	hour	45.00
Survey		
—2 to 3 men	day	250.00
EXCAVATION		
Equipment Rental		
—$^3/_4$ CY backhoe	day	175.00
— 75 HP bulldozer	day	200.00
— 5 CY dump truck	week	500.00
— 2 CY loader	week	1,200.00
Tree & Brush Removal		
— light	acre	500.00
— heavy	acre	1,200.00
— wooded	acre	2,000.00
LABOR		
(Wages, Benefits, Insurance, & Taxes)		
— Bricklayer	hour	21.00
— Bricklayer's Tender	hour	15.50
— Building Laborer	hour	16.50
— Carpenter	hour	21.00
— Cement Mason	hour	20.00
— Drywall Installer	hour	21.00
— Drywall Taper	hour	20.00
— Electrician	hour	22.00
— Floor layer	hour	20.00
— Glazier	hour	20.00
— Lather	hour	21.00
— Marble Setter	hour	19.50
— Mosaic Tile Worker	hour	19.00
— Operating Engineer	hour	23.00
— Painter	hour	20.00
— Plasterer	hour	21.00
— Plasterer's Helper	hour	16.00
— Plumber	hour	23.00
— Reinforcing Ironworker	hour	22.00
— Roofer (composition)	hour	23.00
— Sheet Metal Worker	hour	22.50
— Tile Layer	hour	19.50
— Truck Driver	hour	18.00

Appendix E
Mortgage
Payment Comparisons

These tables will enable the reader to determine the exact amount of a monthly mortgage payment (principal & interest) on amounts financed in the $50,000 through $290,000 range for terms of 15 through 30 years, at interest rates from 5 through $12^{1}/_{2}\%$.

The values used herein were chosen to encompass a majority cross section of the home building populace, taking into account contemporary mortgage vehicles (buydowns), usual terms for payback, and dollar amounts typically financed.

The figures interpolated from the tables do not include escrow accounts set up by lenders to pay insurance premiums and property taxes on the mortgaged property.

MORTGAGE COMPARISON

15 YEAR MORTGAGES

RATES -> AMOUNTS	5.000%	5.500%	6.000%	6.500%	7.000%	7.500%	8.000%	8.500%
50,000.00	395.40	408.54	421.93	435.55	449.41	463.51	477.83	492.37
60,000.00	474.48	490.25	506.31	522.66	539.30	556.21	573.39	590.84
70,000.00	553.56	571.96	590.70	609.78	629.18	648.91	668.96	689.32
80,000.00	632.64	653.67	675.09	696.89	719.06	741.61	764.52	787.79
90,000.00	711.71	735.38	759.47	784.00	808.95	834.31	860.09	886.27
100,000.00	790.79	817.08	843.86	871.11	898.83	927.01	955.65	984.74
110,000.00	869.87	898.79	928.24	958.22	988.71	1,019.71	1,051.22	1,083.21
120,000.00	948.95	980.50	1,012.63	1,045.33	1,078.59	1,112.41	1,146.78	1,181.69
130,000.00	1,028.03	1,062.21	1,097.01	1,132.44	1,168.48	1,205.12	1,242.35	1,280.16
140,000.00	1,107.11	1,143.92	1,181.40	1,219.55	1,258.36	1,297.82	1,337.91	1,378.64
150,000.00	1,186.19	1,225.63	1,265.79	1,306.66	1,348.24	1,390.52	1,433.48	1,477.11
160,000.00	1,265.27	1,307.33	1,350.17	1,393.77	1,438.13	1,483.22	1,529.04	1,575.58
170,000.00	1,344.35	1,389.04	1,434.56	1,480.88	1,528.01	1,575.92	1,624.61	1,674.06
180,000.00	1,423.43	1,470.75	1,518.94	1,567.99	1,617.89	1,668.62	1,720.17	1,772.53
190,000.00	1,502.51	1,552.46	1,603.33	1,655.10	1,707.77	1,761.32	1,815.74	1,871.01
200,000.00	1,581.59	1,634.17	1,687.71	1,742.21	1,797.66	1,854.02	1,911.30	1,969.48
210,000.00	1,660.67	1,715.88	1,772.10	1,829.33	1,887.54	1,946.73	2,006.87	2,067.95
220,000.00	1,739.75	1,797.58	1,856.49	1,916.44	1,977.42	2,039.43	2,102.43	2,166.43
230,000.00	1,818.83	1,879.29	1,940.87	2,003.55	2,067.31	2,132.13	2,198.00	2,264.90
240,000.00	1,897.90	1,961.00	2,025.26	2,090.66	2,157.19	2,224.83	2,293.57	2,363.38
250,000.00	1,976.98	2,042.71	2,109.64	2,177.77	2,247.07	2,317.53	2,389.13	2,461.85
260,000.00	2,056.06	2,124.42	2,194.03	2,264.88	2,336.95	2,410.23	2,484.70	2,560.32
270,000.00	2,135.14	2,206.13	2,278.41	2,351.99	2,426.84	2,502.93	2,580.26	2,658.80
280,000.00	2,214.22	2,287.83	2,362.80	2,439.10	2,516.72	2,595.63	2,675.83	2,757.27
290,000.00	2,293.30	2,369.54	2,447.18	2,526.21	2,606.60	2,688.34	2,771.39	2,855.74

RATES -> AMOUNTS	9.000%	9.500%	10.000%	10.500%	11.000%	11.500%	12.000%	12.500%
50,000.00	507.13	522.11	537.30	552.70	568.30	584.10	600.08	616.26
60,000.00	608.56	626.53	644.76	663.24	681.96	700.91	720.10	739.51
70,000.00	709.99	730.96	752.22	773.78	795.62	817.73	840.12	862.77
80,000.00	811.41	835.38	859.68	884.32	909.28	934.55	960.13	986.02
90,000.00	912.84	939.80	967.14	994.86	1,022.94	1,051.37	1,080.15	1,109.27
100,000.00	1,014.27	1,044.22	1,074.61	1,105.40	1,136.60	1,168.19	1,200.17	1,232.52
110,000.00	1,115.69	1,148.65	1,182.07	1,215.94	1,250.26	1,285.01	1,320.18	1,355.77
120,000.00	1,217.12	1,253.07	1,289.53	1,326.48	1,363.92	1,401.83	1,440.20	1,479.03
130,000.00	1,318.55	1,357.49	1,396.99	1,437.02	1,477.58	1,518.65	1,560.22	1,602.28
140,000.00	1,419.97	1,461.91	1,504.45	1,547.56	1,591.24	1,635.47	1,680.24	1,725.53
150,000.00	1,521.40	1,566.34	1,611.91	1,658.10	1,704.90	1,752.28	1,800.25	1,848.78
160,000.00	1,622.83	1,670.76	1,719.37	1,768.64	1,818.56	1,869.10	1,920.27	1,972.04
170,000.00	1,724.25	1,775.18	1,826.83	1,879.18	1,932.21	1,985.92	2,040.29	2,095.29
180,000.00	1,825.68	1,879.60	1,934.29	1,989.72	2,045.87	2,102.74	2,160.30	2,218.54
190,000.00	1,927.11	1,984.03	2,041.75	2,100.26	2,159.53	2,219.56	2,280.32	2,341.79
200,000.00	2,028.53	2,088.45	2,149.21	2,210.80	2,273.19	2,336.38	2,400.34	2,465.04
210,000.00	2,129.96	2,192.87	2,256.67	2,321.34	2,386.85	2,453.20	2,520.35	2,588.30
220,000.00	2,231.39	2,297.29	2,364.13	2,431.88	2,500.51	2,570.02	2,640.37	2,711.55
230,000.00	2,332.81	2,401.72	2,471.59	2,542.42	2,614.17	2,686.84	2,760.39	2,834.80
240,000.00	2,434.24	2,506.14	2,579.05	2,652.96	2,727.83	2,803.66	2,880.40	2,958.05
250,000.00	2,535.67	2,610.56	2,686.51	2,763.50	2,841.49	2,920.47	3,000.42	3,081.31
260,000.00	2,637.09	2,714.98	2,793.97	2,874.04	2,955.15	3,037.29	3,120.44	3,204.56
270,000.00	2,738.52	2,819.41	2,901.43	2,984.58	3,068.81	3,154.11	3,240.45	3,327.81
280,000.00	2,839.95	2,923.83	3,008.89	3,095.12	3,182.47	3,270.93	3,360.47	3,451.06
290,000.00	2,941.37	3,028.25	3,116.36	3,205.66	3,296.13	3,387.75	3,480.49	3,574.31

MORTGAGE COMPARISON

16 YEAR MORTGAGES

RATES ->	5.000%	5.500%	6.000%	6.500%	7.000%	7.500%	8.000%	8.500%
AMOUNTS								
50,000.00	378.84	392.15	405.72	419.54	433.60	447.91	462.46	477.25
60,000.00	454.61	470.58	486.86	503.45	520.32	537.50	554.96	572.69
70,000.00	530.38	549.01	568.01	587.35	607.05	627.08	647.45	668.14
80,000.00	606.14	627.44	649.15	671.26	693.77	716.66	739.94	763.59
90,000.00	681.91	705.87	730.29	755.17	780.49	806.24	832.43	859.04
100,000.00	757.68	784.30	811.44	839.08	867.21	895.83	924.93	954.49
110,000.00	833.45	862.73	892.58	922.98	953.93	985.41	1,017.42	1,049.94
120,000.00	909.22	941.16	973.73	1,006.89	1,040.65	1,074.99	1,109.91	1,145.39
130,000.00	984.99	1,019.60	1,054.87	1,090.80	1,127.37	1,164.58	1,202.40	1,240.84
140,000.00	1,060.75	1,098.03	1,136.01	1,174.71	1,214.09	1,254.16	1,294.90	1,336.29
150,000.00	1,136.52	1,176.46	1,217.16	1,258.61	1,300.81	1,343.74	1,387.39	1,431.74
160,000.00	1,212.29	1,254.89	1,298.30	1,342.52	1,387.53	1,433.32	1,479.88	1,527.19
170,000.00	1,288.06	1,333.32	1,379.44	1,426.43	1,474.25	1,522.91	1,572.37	1,622.63
180,000.00	1,363.83	1,411.75	1,460.59	1,510.34	1,560.97	1,612.49	1,664.87	1,718.08
190,000.00	1,439.59	1,490.18	1,541.73	1,594.24	1,647.70	1,702.07	1,757.36	1,813.53
200,000.00	1,515.36	1,568.61	1,622.88	1,678.15	1,734.42	1,791.66	1,849.85	1,908.98
210,000.00	1,591.13	1,647.04	1,704.02	1,762.06	1,821.14	1,881.24	1,942.34	2,004.43
220,000.00	1,666.90	1,725.47	1,785.16	1,845.97	1,907.86	1,970.82	2,034.84	2,099.88
230,000.00	1,742.67	1,803.90	1,866.31	1,929.87	1,994.58	2,060.40	2,127.33	2,195.33
240,000.00	1,818.43	1,882.33	1,947.45	2,013.78	2,081.30	2,149.99	2,219.82	2,290.78
250,000.00	1,894.20	1,960.76	2,028.59	2,097.69	2,168.02	2,239.57	2,312.31	2,386.23
260,000.00	1,969.97	2,039.19	2,109.74	2,181.60	2,254.74	2,329.15	2,404.81	2,481.68
270,000.00	2,045.74	2,117.62	2,190.88	2,265.50	2,341.46	2,418.73	2,497.30	2,577.13
280,000.00	2,121.51	2,196.05	2,272.03	2,349.41	2,428.18	2,508.32	2,589.79	2,672.57
290,000.00	2,197.28	2,274.48	2,353.17	2,433.32	2,514.90	2,597.90	2,682.28	2,768.02

RATES ->	9.000%	9.500%	10.000%	10.500%	11.000%	11.500%	12.000%	12.500%
AMOUNTS								
50,000.00	492.26	507.49	522.95	538.62	554.50	570.58	586.86	603.34
60,000.00	590.71	608.99	627.54	646.35	665.40	684.70	704.24	724.00
70,000.00	689.16	710.49	732.13	754.07	776.30	798.82	821.61	844.67
80,000.00	787.61	811.99	836.72	861.79	887.20	912.93	938.98	965.34
90,000.00	886.06	913.49	941.31	969.52	998.10	1,027.05	1,056.35	1,086.00
100,000.00	984.52	1,014.99	1,045.90	1,077.24	1,109.00	1,141.17	1,173.73	1,206.67
110,000.00	1,082.97	1,116.49	1,150.49	1,184.97	1,219.90	1,255.28	1,291.10	1,327.34
120,000.00	1,181.42	1,217.99	1,255.08	1,292.69	1,330.80	1,369.40	1,408.47	1,448.00
130,000.00	1,279.87	1,319.49	1,359.67	1,400.42	1,441.70	1,483.51	1,525.84	1,568.67
140,000.00	1,378.32	1,420.99	1,464.26	1,508.14	1,552.60	1,597.63	1,643.22	1,689.34
150,000.00	1,476.77	1,522.48	1,568.85	1,615.86	1,663.50	1,711.75	1,760.59	1,810.00
160,000.00	1,575.23	1,623.98	1,673.44	1,723.59	1,774.40	1,825.86	1,877.96	1,930.67
170,000.00	1,673.68	1,725.48	1,778.03	1,831.31	1,885.30	1,939.98	1,995.33	2,051.34
180,000.00	1,772.13	1,826.98	1,882.62	1,939.04	1,996.20	2,054.10	2,112.71	2,172.01
190,000.00	1,870.58	1,928.48	1,987.21	2,046.76	2,107.10	2,168.21	2,230.08	2,292.67
200,000.00	1,969.03	2,029.98	2,091.80	2,154.48	2,218.00	2,282.33	2,347.45	2,413.34
210,000.00	2,067.48	2,131.48	2,196.39	2,262.21	2,328.90	2,396.45	2,464.82	2,534.01
220,000.00	2,165.93	2,232.98	2,300.98	2,369.93	2,439.80	2,510.56	2,582.20	2,654.67
230,000.00	2,264.39	2,334.48	2,405.57	2,477.66	2,550.70	2,624.68	2,699.57	2,775.34
240,000.00	2,362.84	2,435.98	2,510.16	2,585.38	2,661.60	2,738.80	2,816.94	2,896.01
250,000.00	2,461.29	2,537.47	2,614.76	2,693.11	2,772.50	2,852.91	2,934.31	3,016.67
260,000.00	2,559.74	2,638.97	2,719.35	2,800.83	2,883.40	2,967.03	3,051.69	3,137.34
270,000.00	2,658.19	2,740.47	2,823.94	2,908.55	2,994.30	3,081.15	3,169.06	3,258.01
280,000.00	2,756.64	2,841.97	2,928.53	3,016.28	3,105.20	3,195.26	3,286.43	3,378.68
290,000.00	2,855.10	2,943.47	3,033.12	3,124.00	3,216.10	3,309.38	3,403.80	3,499.34

MORTGAGE COMPARISON
17 YEAR MORTGAGES

RATES -> AMOUNTS	5.000%	5.500%	6.000%	6.500%	7.000%	7.500%	8.000%	8.500%
50,000.00	364.33	377.80	391.55	405.56	419.83	434.35	449.13	464.15
60,000.00	437.19	453.37	469.86	486.67	503.80	521.23	538.95	556.98
70,000.00	510.06	528.93	548.17	567.78	587.76	608.10	628.78	649.80
80,000.00	582.92	604.49	626.48	648.90	671.73	694.97	718.61	742.63
90,000.00	655.79	680.05	704.79	730.01	755.69	781.84	808.43	835.46
100,000.00	728.66	755.61	783.10	811.12	839.66	868.71	898.26	928.29
110,000.00	801.52	831.17	861.41	892.23	923.63	955.58	988.08	1,021.12
120,000.00	874.39	906.73	939.72	973.35	1,007.59	1,042.45	1,077.91	1,113.95
130,000.00	947.25	982.29	1,018.03	1,054.46	1,091.56	1,129.32	1,167.73	1,206.78
140,000.00	1,020.12	1,057.85	1,096.34	1,135.57	1,175.53	1,216.19	1,257.56	1,299.61
150,000.00	1,092.98	1,133.41	1,174.65	1,216.68	1,259.49	1,303.06	1,347.39	1,392.44
160,000.00	1,165.85	1,208.97	1,252.96	1,297.79	1,343.46	1,389.94	1,437.21	1,485.27
170,000.00	1,238.71	1,284.54	1,331.27	1,378.91	1,427.42	1,476.81	1,527.04	1,578.10
180,000.00	1,311.58	1,360.10	1,409.58	1,460.02	1,511.39	1,563.68	1,616.86	1,670.93
190,000.00	1,384.45	1,435.66	1,487.89	1,541.13	1,595.36	1,650.55	1,706.69	1,763.76
200,000.00	1,457.31	1,511.22	1,566.20	1,622.24	1,679.32	1,737.42	1,796.51	1,856.58
210,000.00	1,530.18	1,586.78	1,644.51	1,703.35	1,763.29	1,824.29	1,886.34	1,949.41
220,000.00	1,603.04	1,662.34	1,722.82	1,784.47	1,847.25	1,911.16	1,976.17	2,042.24
230,000.00	1,675.91	1,737.90	1,801.13	1,865.58	1,931.22	1,998.03	2,065.99	2,135.07
240,000.00	1,748.77	1,813.46	1,879.44	1,946.69	2,015.19	2,084.90	2,155.82	2,227.90
250,000.00	1,821.64	1,889.02	1,957.75	2,027.80	2,099.15	2,171.77	2,245.64	2,320.73
260,000.00	1,894.50	1,964.58	2,036.06	2,108.91	2,183.12	2,258.64	2,335.47	2,413.56
270,000.00	1,967.37	2,040.14	2,114.37	2,190.03	2,267.08	2,345.52	2,425.29	2,506.39
280,000.00	2,040.23	2,115.71	2,192.68	2,271.14	2,351.05	2,432.39	2,515.12	2,599.22
290,000.00	2,113.10	2,191.27	2,270.99	2,352.25	2,435.02	2,519.26	2,604.94	2,692.05

RATES -> AMOUNTS	9.000%	9.500%	10.000%	10.500%	11.000%	11.500%	12.000%	12.500%
50,000.00	479.40	494.89	510.61	526.54	542.69	559.05	575.61	592.36
60,000.00	575.28	593.87	612.73	631.85	651.23	670.86	690.73	710.84
70,000.00	671.16	692.85	714.85	737.16	759.77	782.67	805.85	829.31
80,000.00	767.04	791.82	816.97	842.47	868.30	894.48	920.97	947.78
90,000.00	862.92	890.80	919.09	947.77	976.84	1,006.29	1,036.09	1,066.25
100,000.00	958.80	989.78	1,021.21	1,053.08	1,085.38	1,118.10	1,151.22	1,184.73
110,000.00	1,054.68	1,088.76	1,123.33	1,158.39	1,193.92	1,229.91	1,266.34	1,303.20
120,000.00	1,150.56	1,187.74	1,225.45	1,263.70	1,302.46	1,341.72	1,381.46	1,421.67
130,000.00	1,246.45	1,286.71	1,327.57	1,369.01	1,410.99	1,453.53	1,496.58	1,540.14
140,000.00	1,342.33	1,385.69	1,429.69	1,474.31	1,519.53	1,565.33	1,611.70	1,658.62
150,000.00	1,438.21	1,484.67	1,531.82	1,579.62	1,628.07	1,677.14	1,726.82	1,777.09
160,000.00	1,534.09	1,583.65	1,633.94	1,684.93	1,736.61	1,788.95	1,841.94	1,895.56
170,000.00	1,629.97	1,682.63	1,736.06	1,790.24	1,845.15	1,900.76	1,957.07	2,014.03
180,000.00	1,725.85	1,781.61	1,838.18	1,895.55	1,953.69	2,012.57	2,072.19	2,132.51
190,000.00	1,821.73	1,880.58	1,940.30	2,000.85	2,062.22	2,124.38	2,187.31	2,250.98
200,000.00	1,917.61	1,979.56	2,042.42	2,106.16	2,170.76	2,236.19	2,302.43	2,369.45
210,000.00	2,013.49	2,078.54	2,144.54	2,211.47	2,279.30	2,348.00	2,417.55	2,487.92
220,000.00	2,109.37	2,177.52	2,246.66	2,316.78	2,387.84	2,459.81	2,532.67	2,606.40
230,000.00	2,205.25	2,276.50	2,348.78	2,422.09	2,496.38	2,571.62	2,647.80	2,724.87
240,000.00	2,301.13	2,375.47	2,450.91	2,527.40	2,604.91	2,683.43	2,762.92	2,843.34
250,000.00	2,397.01	2,474.45	2,553.03	2,632.70	2,713.45	2,795.24	2,878.04	2,961.81
260,000.00	2,492.89	2,573.43	2,655.15	2,738.01	2,821.99	2,907.05	2,993.16	3,080.29
270,000.00	2,588.77	2,672.41	2,757.27	2,843.32	2,930.53	3,018.86	3,108.28	3,198.76
280,000.00	2,684.65	2,771.39	2,859.39	2,948.63	3,039.07	3,130.67	3,223.40	3,317.23
290,000.00	2,780.53	2,870.36	2,961.51	3,053.94	3,147.60	3,242.48	3,338.53	3,435.70

MORTGAGE   COMPARISON

18   YEAR   MORTGAGES

RATES -> AMOUNTS	5.000%	5.500%	6.000%	6.500%	7.000%	7.500%	8.000%	8.500%
50,000.00	351.52	365.16	379.08	393.28	407.75	422.49	437.48	452.73
60,000.00	421.82	438.19	454.90	471.94	489.30	506.98	524.98	543.27
70,000.00	492.12	511.22	530.71	550.59	570.85	591.48	612.47	633.82
80,000.00	562.43	584.25	606.53	629.25	652.40	675.98	699.97	724.37
90,000.00	632.73	657.28	682.35	707.91	733.95	760.48	787.47	814.91
100,000.00	703.03	730.32	758.16	786.56	815.50	844.97	874.96	905.46
110,000.00	773.34	803.35	833.98	865.22	897.05	929.47	962.46	996.00
120,000.00	843.64	876.38	909.79	943.87	978.60	1,013.97	1,049.96	1,086.55
130,000.00	913.94	949.41	985.61	1,022.53	1,060.15	1,098.47	1,137.45	1,177.09
140,000.00	984.25	1,022.44	1,061.43	1,101.19	1,141.70	1,182.96	1,224.95	1,267.64
150,000.00	1,054.55	1,095.47	1,137.24	1,179.84	1,223.25	1,267.46	1,312.44	1,358.19
160,000.00	1,124.85	1,168.51	1,213.06	1,258.50	1,304.80	1,351.96	1,399.94	1,448.73
170,000.00	1,195.16	1,241.54	1,288.88	1,337.15	1,386.35	1,436.45	1,487.44	1,539.28
180,000.00	1,265.46	1,314.57	1,364.69	1,415.81	1,467.90	1,520.95	1,574.93	1,629.82
190,000.00	1,335.76	1,387.60	1,440.51	1,494.47	1,549.45	1,605.45	1,662.43	1,720.37
200,000.00	1,406.07	1,460.63	1,516.32	1,573.12	1,631.00	1,689.95	1,749.93	1,810.92
210,000.00	1,476.37	1,533.66	1,592.14	1,651.78	1,712.55	1,774.44	1,837.42	1,901.46
220,000.00	1,546.67	1,606.70	1,667.96	1,730.43	1,794.10	1,858.94	1,924.92	1,992.01
230,000.00	1,616.98	1,679.73	1,743.77	1,809.09	1,875.66	1,943.44	2,012.41	2,082.55
240,000.00	1,687.28	1,752.76	1,819.59	1,887.75	1,957.21	2,027.94	2,099.91	2,173.10
250,000.00	1,757.58	1,825.79	1,895.41	1,966.40	2,038.76	2,112.43	2,187.41	2,263.64
260,000.00	1,827.89	1,898.82	1,971.22	2,045.06	2,120.31	2,196.93	2,274.90	2,354.19
270,000.00	1,898.19	1,971.85	2,047.04	2,123.72	2,201.86	2,281.43	2,362.40	2,444.74
280,000.00	1,968.49	2,044.89	2,122.85	2,202.37	2,283.41	2,365.93	2,449.90	2,535.28
290,000.00	2,038.80	2,117.92	2,198.67	2,281.03	2,364.96	2,450.42	2,537.39	2,625.83

RATES -> AMOUNTS	9.000%	9.500%	10.000%	10.500%	11.000%	11.500%	12.000%	12.500%
50,000.00	468.22	483.96	499.92	516.11	532.52	549.15	565.98	583.00
60,000.00	561.87	580.75	599.91	619.34	639.03	658.98	679.17	699.60
70,000.00	655.51	677.54	699.89	722.56	745.53	768.81	792.37	816.20
80,000.00	749.16	774.33	799.88	825.78	852.04	878.64	905.56	932.80
90,000.00	842.80	871.12	899.86	929.01	958.54	988.47	1,018.76	1,049.40
100,000.00	936.44	967.91	999.84	1,032.23	1,065.05	1,098.30	1,131.95	1,166.00
110,000.00	1,030.09	1,064.70	1,099.83	1,135.45	1,171.55	1,208.12	1,245.15	1,282.60
120,000.00	1,123.73	1,161.49	1,199.81	1,238.67	1,278.06	1,317.95	1,358.34	1,399.20
130,000.00	1,217.38	1,258.28	1,299.80	1,341.90	1,384.56	1,427.78	1,471.54	1,515.80
140,000.00	1,311.02	1,355.08	1,399.78	1,445.12	1,491.07	1,537.61	1,584.73	1,632.40
150,000.00	1,404.67	1,451.87	1,499.77	1,548.34	1,597.57	1,647.44	1,697.93	1,749.00
160,000.00	1,498.31	1,548.66	1,599.75	1,651.56	1,704.08	1,757.27	1,811.12	1,865.60
170,000.00	1,591.96	1,645.45	1,699.73	1,754.79	1,810.58	1,867.10	1,924.32	1,982.20
180,000.00	1,685.60	1,742.24	1,799.72	1,858.01	1,917.09	1,976.93	2,037.51	2,098.80
190,000.00	1,779.25	1,839.03	1,899.70	1,961.23	2,023.59	2,086.76	2,150.71	2,215.40
200,000.00	1,872.89	1,935.82	1,999.69	2,064.46	2,130.10	2,196.59	2,263.90	2,332.00
210,000.00	1,966.53	2,032.61	2,099.67	2,167.68	2,236.60	2,306.42	2,377.10	2,448.60
220,000.00	2,060.18	2,129.41	2,199.66	2,270.90	2,343.11	2,416.25	2,490.29	2,565.20
230,000.00	2,153.82	2,226.20	2,299.64	2,374.12	2,449.61	2,526.08	2,603.49	2,681.80
240,000.00	2,247.47	2,322.99	2,399.63	2,477.35	2,556.12	2,635.91	2,716.68	2,798.40
250,000.00	2,341.11	2,419.78	2,499.61	2,580.57	2,662.62	2,745.74	2,829.88	2,915.00
260,000.00	2,434.76	2,516.57	2,599.59	2,683.79	2,769.13	2,855.57	2,943.07	3,031.60
270,000.00	2,528.40	2,613.36	2,699.58	2,787.02	2,875.63	2,965.40	3,056.27	3,148.20
280,000.00	2,622.05	2,710.15	2,799.56	2,890.24	2,982.14	3,075.23	3,169.46	3,264.80
290,000.00	2,715.69	2,806.94	2,899.55	2,993.46	3,088.64	3,185.06	3,282.66	3,381.40

MORTGAGE COMPARISON
19 YEAR MORTGAGES

RATES -> AMOUNTS	5.000%	5.500%	6.000%	6.500%	7.000%	7.500%	8.000%	8.500%
50,000.00	340.14	353.94	368.04	382.43	397.10	412.04	427.25	442.72
60,000.00	408.17	424.73	441.65	458.91	476.52	494.45	512.70	531.27
70,000.00	476.19	495.52	515.26	535.40	555.93	576.86	598.15	619.81
80,000.00	544.22	566.31	588.87	611.88	635.35	659.26	683.60	708.36
90,000.00	612.25	637.10	662.47	688.37	714.77	741.67	769.05	796.90
100,000.00	680.28	707.89	736.08	764.86	794.19	824.08	854.50	885.45
110,000.00	748.31	778.67	809.69	841.34	873.61	906.49	939.95	973.99
120,000.00	816.33	849.46	883.30	917.83	953.03	988.89	1,025.40	1,062.53
130,000.00	884.36	920.25	956.91	994.31	1,032.45	1,071.30	1,110.85	1,151.08
140,000.00	952.39	991.04	1,030.52	1,070.80	1,111.87	1,153.71	1,196.30	1,239.62
150,000.00	1,020.42	1,061.83	1,104.12	1,147.28	1,191.29	1,236.12	1,281.75	1,328.17
160,000.00	1,088.44	1,132.62	1,177.73	1,223.77	1,270.71	1,318.53	1,367.20	1,416.71
170,000.00	1,156.47	1,203.41	1,251.34	1,300.26	1,350.13	1,400.93	1,452.65	1,505.26
180,000.00	1,224.50	1,274.20	1,324.95	1,376.74	1,429.55	1,483.34	1,538.10	1,593.80
190,000.00	1,292.53	1,344.98	1,398.56	1,453.23	1,508.97	1,565.75	1,623.55	1,682.35
200,000.00	1,360.56	1,415.77	1,472.17	1,529.71	1,588.38	1,648.16	1,709.00	1,770.89
210,000.00	1,428.58	1,486.56	1,545.77	1,606.20	1,667.80	1,730.57	1,794.45	1,859.44
220,000.00	1,496.61	1,557.35	1,619.38	1,682.68	1,747.22	1,812.97	1,879.90	1,947.98
230,000.00	1,564.64	1,628.14	1,692.99	1,759.17	1,826.64	1,895.38	1,965.35	2,036.53
240,000.00	1,632.67	1,698.93	1,766.60	1,835.65	1,906.06	1,977.79	2,050.80	2,125.07
250,000.00	1,700.69	1,769.72	1,840.21	1,912.14	1,985.48	2,060.20	2,136.25	2,213.61
260,000.00	1,768.72	1,840.50	1,913.82	1,988.63	2,064.90	2,142.61	2,221.70	2,302.16
270,000.00	1,836.75	1,911.29	1,987.42	2,065.11	2,144.32	2,225.01	2,307.15	2,390.70
280,000.00	1,904.78	1,982.08	2,061.03	2,141.60	2,223.74	2,307.42	2,392.60	2,479.25
290,000.00	1,972.81	2,052.87	2,134.64	2,218.08	2,303.16	2,389.83	2,478.05	2,567.79

RATES -> AMOUNTS	9.000%	9.500%	10.000%	10.500%	11.000%	11.500%	12.000%	12.500%
50,000.00	458.45	474.42	490.63	507.07	523.73	540.61	557.69	574.98
60,000.00	550.14	569.30	588.76	608.48	628.48	648.73	669.23	689.97
70,000.00	641.83	664.19	686.88	709.90	733.22	756.85	780.77	804.97
80,000.00	733.52	759.07	785.01	811.31	837.97	864.97	892.31	919.96
90,000.00	825.21	853.96	883.13	912.73	942.72	973.10	1,003.85	1,034.96
100,000.00	916.90	948.84	981.26	1,014.14	1,047.46	1,081.22	1,115.39	1,149.95
110,000.00	1,008.59	1,043.72	1,079.38	1,115.55	1,152.21	1,189.34	1,226.92	1,264.95
120,000.00	1,100.28	1,138.61	1,177.51	1,216.97	1,256.96	1,297.46	1,338.46	1,379.94
130,000.00	1,191.97	1,233.49	1,275.64	1,318.38	1,361.70	1,405.58	1,450.00	1,494.94
140,000.00	1,283.66	1,328.38	1,373.76	1,419.79	1,466.45	1,513.71	1,561.54	1,609.93
150,000.00	1,375.35	1,423.26	1,471.89	1,521.21	1,571.20	1,621.83	1,673.08	1,724.93
160,000.00	1,467.03	1,518.14	1,570.01	1,622.62	1,675.94	1,729.95	1,784.62	1,839.92
170,000.00	1,558.72	1,613.03	1,668.14	1,724.04	1,780.69	1,838.07	1,896.16	1,954.92
180,000.00	1,650.41	1,707.91	1,766.27	1,825.45	1,885.44	1,946.19	2,007.69	2,069.91
190,000.00	1,742.10	1,802.80	1,864.39	1,926.86	1,990.18	2,054.31	2,119.23	2,184.91
200,000.00	1,833.79	1,897.68	1,962.52	2,028.28	2,094.93	2,162.44	2,230.77	2,299.90
210,000.00	1,925.48	1,992.56	2,060.64	2,129.69	2,199.67	2,270.56	2,342.31	2,414.90
220,000.00	2,017.17	2,087.45	2,158.77	2,231.11	2,304.42	2,378.68	2,453.85	2,529.89
230,000.00	2,108.86	2,182.33	2,256.90	2,332.52	2,409.17	2,486.80	2,565.39	2,644.89
240,000.00	2,200.55	2,277.22	2,355.02	2,433.93	2,513.91	2,594.92	2,676.93	2,759.88
250,000.00	2,292.24	2,372.10	2,453.15	2,535.35	2,618.66	2,703.05	2,788.46	2,874.88
260,000.00	2,383.93	2,466.98	2,551.27	2,636.76	2,723.41	2,811.17	2,900.00	2,989.87
270,000.00	2,475.62	2,561.87	2,649.40	2,738.18	2,828.15	2,919.29	3,011.54	3,104.87
280,000.00	2,567.31	2,656.75	2,747.53	2,839.59	2,932.90	3,027.41	3,123.08	3,219.86
290,000.00	2,659.00	2,751.64	2,845.65	2,941.00	3,037.65	3,135.53	3,234.62	3,334.86

MORTGAGE COMPARISON
20 YEAR MORTGAGES

RATES -> AMOUNTS	5.000%	5.500%	6.000%	6.500%	7.000%	7.500%	8.000%	8.500%
50,000.00	329.98	343.94	358.22	372.79	387.65	402.80	418.22	433.91
60,000.00	395.97	412.73	429.86	447.34	465.18	483.36	501.86	520.69
70,000.00	461.97	481.52	501.50	521.90	542.71	563.92	585.51	607.48
80,000.00	527.96	550.31	573.14	596.46	620.24	644.47	669.15	694.26
90,000.00	593.96	619.10	644.79	671.02	697.77	725.03	752.80	781.04
100,000.00	659.96	687.89	716.43	745.57	775.30	805.59	836.44	867.82
110,000.00	725.95	756.68	788.07	820.13	852.83	886.15	920.08	954.61
120,000.00	791.95	825.46	859.72	894.69	930.36	966.71	1,003.73	1,041.39
130,000.00	857.94	894.25	931.36	969.25	1,007.89	1,047.27	1,087.37	1,128.17
140,000.00	923.94	963.04	1,003.00	1,043.80	1,085.42	1,127.83	1,171.02	1,214.95
150,000.00	989.93	1,031.83	1,074.65	1,118.36	1,162.95	1,208.39	1,254.66	1,301.73
160,000.00	1,055.93	1,100.62	1,146.29	1,192.92	1,240.48	1,288.95	1,338.30	1,388.52
170,000.00	1,121.92	1,169.41	1,217.93	1,267.47	1,318.01	1,369.51	1,421.95	1,475.30
180,000.00	1,187.92	1,238.20	1,289.58	1,342.03	1,395.54	1,450.07	1,505.59	1,562.08
190,000.00	1,253.92	1,306.99	1,361.22	1,416.59	1,473.07	1,530.63	1,589.24	1,648.86
200,000.00	1,319.91	1,375.77	1,432.86	1,491.15	1,550.60	1,611.19	1,672.88	1,735.65
210,000.00	1,385.91	1,444.56	1,504.51	1,565.70	1,628.13	1,691.75	1,756.52	1,822.43
220,000.00	1,451.90	1,513.35	1,576.15	1,640.26	1,705.66	1,772.31	1,840.17	1,909.21
230,000.00	1,517.90	1,582.14	1,647.79	1,714.82	1,783.19	1,852.86	1,923.81	1,995.99
240,000.00	1,583.89	1,650.93	1,719.43	1,789.38	1,860.72	1,933.42	2,007.46	2,082.78
250,000.00	1,649.89	1,719.72	1,791.08	1,863.93	1,938.25	2,013.98	2,091.10	2,169.56
260,000.00	1,715.89	1,788.51	1,862.72	1,938.49	2,015.78	2,094.54	2,174.74	2,256.34
270,000.00	1,781.88	1,857.30	1,934.36	2,013.05	2,093.31	2,175.10	2,258.39	2,343.12
280,000.00	1,847.88	1,926.08	2,006.01	2,087.60	2,170.84	2,255.66	2,342.03	2,429.91
290,000.00	1,913.87	1,994.87	2,077.65	2,162.16	2,248.37	2,336.22	2,425.68	2,516.69

RATES -> AMOUNTS	9.000%	9.500%	10.000%	10.500%	11.000%	11.500%	12.000%	12.500%
50,000.00	449.86	466.07	482.51	499.19	516.09	533.21	550.54	568.07
60,000.00	539.84	559.28	579.01	599.03	619.31	639.86	660.65	681.68
70,000.00	629.81	652.49	675.52	698.87	722.53	746.50	770.76	795.30
80,000.00	719.78	745.71	772.02	798.70	825.75	853.14	880.87	908.91
90,000.00	809.75	838.92	868.52	898.54	928.97	959.79	990.98	1,022.53
100,000.00	899.73	932.13	965.02	998.38	1,032.19	1,066.43	1,101.09	1,136.14
110,000.00	989.70	1,025.34	1,061.52	1,098.22	1,135.41	1,173.07	1,211.19	1,249.75
120,000.00	1,079.67	1,118.56	1,158.03	1,198.06	1,238.63	1,279.72	1,321.30	1,363.37
130,000.00	1,169.64	1,211.77	1,254.53	1,297.89	1,341.84	1,386.36	1,431.41	1,476.98
140,000.00	1,259.62	1,304.98	1,351.03	1,397.73	1,445.06	1,493.00	1,541.52	1,590.60
150,000.00	1,349.59	1,398.20	1,447.53	1,497.57	1,548.28	1,599.64	1,651.63	1,704.21
160,000.00	1,439.56	1,491.41	1,544.03	1,597.41	1,651.50	1,706.29	1,761.74	1,817.83
170,000.00	1,529.53	1,584.62	1,640.54	1,697.25	1,754.72	1,812.93	1,871.85	1,931.44
180,000.00	1,619.51	1,677.84	1,737.04	1,797.08	1,857.94	1,919.57	1,981.96	2,045.05
190,000.00	1,709.48	1,771.05	1,833.54	1,896.92	1,961.16	2,026.22	2,092.06	2,158.67
200,000.00	1,799.45	1,864.26	1,930.04	1,996.76	2,064.38	2,132.86	2,202.17	2,272.28
210,000.00	1,889.42	1,957.48	2,026.55	2,096.60	2,167.60	2,239.50	2,312.28	2,385.90
220,000.00	1,979.40	2,050.69	2,123.05	2,196.44	2,270.81	2,346.15	2,422.39	2,499.51
230,000.00	2,069.37	2,143.90	2,219.55	2,296.27	2,374.03	2,452.79	2,532.50	2,613.12
240,000.00	2,159.34	2,237.11	2,316.05	2,396.11	2,477.25	2,559.43	2,642.61	2,726.74
250,000.00	2,249.31	2,330.33	2,412.55	2,495.95	2,580.47	2,666.07	2,752.72	2,840.35
260,000.00	2,339.29	2,423.54	2,509.06	2,595.79	2,683.69	2,772.72	2,862.82	2,953.97
270,000.00	2,429.26	2,516.75	2,605.56	2,695.63	2,786.91	2,879.36	2,972.93	3,067.58
280,000.00	2,519.23	2,609.97	2,702.06	2,795.46	2,890.13	2,986.00	3,083.04	3,181.19
290,000.00	2,609.21	2,703.18	2,798.56	2,895.30	2,993.35	3,092.65	3,193.15	3,294.81

MORTGAGE COMPARISON

21 YEAR MORTGAGES

RATES -> AMOUNTS	5.000%	5.500%	6.000%	6.500%	7.000%	7.500%	8.000%	8.500%
50,000.00	320.86	334.99	349.43	364.18	379.24	394.58	410.21	426.12
60,000.00	385.03	401.98	419.31	437.02	455.08	473.50	492.26	511.34
70,000.00	449.20	468.98	489.20	509.85	530.93	552.42	574.30	596.57
80,000.00	513.38	535.98	559.09	582.69	606.78	631.33	656.34	681.79
90,000.00	577.55	602.97	628.97	655.53	682.62	710.25	738.39	767.02
100,000.00	641.72	669.97	698.86	728.36	758.47	789.17	820.43	852.24
110,000.00	705.89	736.97	768.74	801.20	834.32	868.08	902.47	937.46
120,000.00	770.06	803.96	838.63	874.04	910.17	947.00	984.51	1,022.69
130,000.00	834.23	870.96	908.51	946.87	986.01	1,025.92	1,066.56	1,107.91
140,000.00	898.41	937.96	978.40	1,019.71	1,061.86	1,104.83	1,148.60	1,193.14
150,000.00	962.58	1,004.96	1,048.29	1,092.54	1,137.71	1,183.75	1,230.64	1,278.36
160,000.00	1,026.75	1,071.95	1,118.17	1,165.38	1,213.55	1,262.67	1,312.68	1,363.58
170,000.00	1,090.92	1,138.95	1,188.06	1,238.22	1,289.40	1,341.58	1,394.73	1,448.81
180,000.00	1,155.09	1,205.95	1,257.94	1,311.05	1,365.25	1,420.50	1,476.77	1,534.03
190,000.00	1,219.27	1,272.94	1,327.83	1,383.89	1,441.10	1,499.42	1,558.81	1,619.25
200,000.00	1,283.44	1,339.94	1,397.71	1,456.73	1,516.94	1,578.33	1,640.86	1,704.48
210,000.00	1,347.61	1,406.94	1,467.60	1,529.56	1,592.79	1,657.25	1,722.90	1,789.70
220,000.00	1,411.78	1,473.93	1,537.49	1,602.40	1,668.64	1,736.17	1,804.94	1,874.93
230,000.00	1,475.95	1,540.93	1,607.37	1,675.23	1,744.49	1,815.08	1,886.98	1,960.15
240,000.00	1,540.12	1,607.93	1,677.26	1,748.07	1,820.33	1,894.00	1,969.03	2,045.37
250,000.00	1,604.30	1,674.93	1,747.14	1,820.91	1,896.18	1,972.92	2,051.07	2,130.60
260,000.00	1,668.47	1,741.92	1,817.03	1,893.74	1,972.03	2,051.83	2,133.11	2,215.82
270,000.00	1,732.64	1,808.92	1,886.91	1,966.58	2,047.87	2,130.75	2,215.16	2,301.05
280,000.00	1,796.81	1,875.92	1,956.80	2,039.42	2,123.72	2,209.66	2,297.20	2,386.27
290,000.00	1,860.98	1,942.91	2,026.69	2,112.25	2,199.57	2,288.58	2,379.24	2,471.49

RATES -> AMOUNTS	9.000%	9.500%	10.000%	10.500%	11.000%	11.500%	12.000%	12.500%
50,000.00	442.29	458.72	475.39	492.30	509.44	526.79	544.35	562.11
60,000.00	530.75	550.46	570.47	590.76	611.32	632.15	653.22	674.53
70,000.00	619.21	642.20	665.55	689.22	713.21	737.50	762.09	786.95
80,000.00	707.66	733.95	760.62	787.68	815.10	842.86	870.96	899.37
90,000.00	796.12	825.69	855.70	886.14	916.98	948.22	979.83	1,011.80
100,000.00	884.58	917.43	950.78	984.60	1,018.87	1,053.58	1,088.70	1,124.22
110,000.00	973.04	1,009.18	1,045.86	1,083.06	1,120.76	1,158.94	1,197.57	1,236.64
120,000.00	1,061.50	1,100.92	1,140.94	1,181.52	1,222.65	1,264.29	1,306.44	1,349.06
130,000.00	1,149.96	1,192.66	1,236.01	1,279.98	1,324.53	1,369.65	1,415.31	1,461.48
140,000.00	1,238.41	1,284.41	1,331.09	1,378.44	1,426.42	1,475.01	1,524.18	1,573.91
150,000.00	1,326.87	1,376.15	1,426.17	1,476.90	1,528.31	1,580.37	1,633.05	1,686.33
160,000.00	1,415.33	1,467.90	1,521.25	1,575.36	1,630.19	1,685.72	1,741.92	1,798.75
170,000.00	1,503.79	1,559.64	1,616.33	1,673.82	1,732.08	1,791.08	1,850.79	1,911.17
180,000.00	1,592.25	1,651.38	1,711.40	1,772.28	1,833.97	1,896.44	1,959.66	2,023.59
190,000.00	1,680.70	1,743.13	1,806.48	1,870.74	1,935.85	2,001.80	2,068.53	2,136.01
200,000.00	1,769.16	1,834.87	1,901.56	1,969.20	2,037.74	2,107.16	2,177.40	2,248.44
210,000.00	1,857.62	1,926.61	1,996.64	2,067.66	2,139.63	2,212.51	2,286.27	2,360.86
220,000.00	1,946.08	2,018.36	2,091.72	2,166.12	2,241.52	2,317.87	2,395.14	2,473.28
230,000.00	2,034.54	2,110.10	2,186.79	2,264.58	2,343.40	2,423.23	2,504.01	2,585.70
240,000.00	2,122.99	2,201.84	2,281.87	2,363.04	2,445.29	2,528.59	2,612.88	2,698.12
250,000.00	2,211.45	2,293.59	2,376.95	2,461.50	2,547.18	2,633.94	2,721.75	2,810.55
260,000.00	2,299.91	2,385.33	2,472.03	2,559.96	2,649.06	2,739.30	2,830.62	2,922.97
270,000.00	2,388.37	2,477.07	2,567.11	2,658.42	2,750.95	2,844.66	2,939.49	3,035.39
280,000.00	2,476.83	2,568.82	2,662.18	2,756.88	2,852.84	2,950.02	3,048.36	3,147.81
290,000.00	2,565.29	2,660.56	2,757.26	2,855.34	2,954.73	3,055.38	3,157.23	3,260.23

MORTGAGE COMPARISON

22 YEAR MORTGAGES

RATES -> AMOUNTS	5.000%	5.500%	6.000%	6.500%	7.000%	7.500%	8.000%	8.500%
50,000.00	312.64	326.92	341.54	356.47	371.71	387.26	403.09	419.20
60,000.00	375.17	392.31	409.84	427.76	446.05	464.71	483.71	503.04
70,000.00	437.70	457.69	478.15	499.06	520.40	542.16	564.32	586.88
80,000.00	500.22	523.08	546.46	570.35	594.74	619.61	644.94	670.73
90,000.00	562.75	588.46	614.77	641.65	669.08	697.06	725.56	754.57
100,000.00	625.28	653.85	683.07	712.94	743.42	774.51	806.18	838.41
110,000.00	687.81	719.23	751.38	784.23	817.77	851.96	886.80	922.25
120,000.00	750.34	784.62	819.69	855.53	892.11	929.41	967.41	1,006.09
130,000.00	812.87	850.00	888.00	926.82	966.45	1,006.86	1,048.03	1,089.93
140,000.00	875.39	915.39	956.30	998.11	1,040.79	1,084.31	1,128.65	1,173.77
150,000.00	937.92	980.77	1,024.61	1,069.41	1,115.14	1,161.77	1,209.27	1,257.61
160,000.00	1,000.45	1,046.16	1,092.92	1,140.70	1,189.48	1,239.22	1,289.88	1,341.45
170,000.00	1,062.98	1,111.54	1,161.23	1,212.00	1,263.82	1,316.67	1,370.50	1,425.29
180,000.00	1,125.51	1,176.93	1,229.53	1,283.29	1,338.16	1,394.12	1,451.12	1,509.13
190,000.00	1,188.03	1,242.31	1,297.84	1,354.58	1,412.51	1,471.57	1,531.74	1,592.97
200,000.00	1,250.56	1,307.70	1,366.15	1,425.88	1,486.85	1,549.02	1,612.36	1,676.81
210,000.00	1,313.09	1,373.08	1,434.46	1,497.17	1,561.19	1,626.47	1,692.97	1,760.65
220,000.00	1,375.62	1,438.47	1,502.76	1,568.47	1,635.53	1,703.92	1,773.59	1,844.49
230,000.00	1,438.15	1,503.85	1,571.07	1,639.76	1,709.88	1,781.37	1,854.21	1,928.33
240,000.00	1,500.67	1,569.24	1,639.38	1,711.05	1,784.22	1,858.83	1,934.83	2,012.17
250,000.00	1,563.20	1,634.62	1,707.69	1,782.35	1,858.56	1,936.28	2,015.44	2,096.02
260,000.00	1,625.73	1,700.01	1,775.99	1,853.64	1,932.90	2,013.73	2,096.06	2,179.86
270,000.00	1,688.26	1,765.39	1,844.30	1,924.94	2,007.25	2,091.18	2,176.68	2,263.70
280,000.00	1,750.79	1,830.78	1,912.61	1,996.23	2,081.59	2,168.63	2,257.30	2,347.54
290,000.00	1,813.31	1,896.16	1,980.92	2,067.52	2,155.93	2,246.08	2,337.92	2,431.38

RATES -> AMOUNTS	9.000%	9.500%	10.000%	10.500%	11.000%	11.500%	12.000%	12.500%
50,000.00	435.59	452.23	469.12	486.25	503.61	521.19	538.97	556.95
60,000.00	522.70	542.68	562.95	583.50	604.33	625.42	646.76	668.34
70,000.00	609.82	633.12	656.77	680.76	705.06	729.66	754.56	779.73
80,000.00	696.94	723.57	750.60	778.01	805.78	833.90	862.35	891.12
90,000.00	784.06	814.02	844.42	875.26	906.50	938.14	970.14	1,002.51
100,000.00	871.17	904.46	938.25	972.51	1,007.22	1,042.37	1,077.94	1,113.90
110,000.00	958.29	994.91	1,032.07	1,069.76	1,107.95	1,146.61	1,185.73	1,225.29
120,000.00	1,045.41	1,085.35	1,125.90	1,167.01	1,208.67	1,250.85	1,293.53	1,336.68
130,000.00	1,132.53	1,175.80	1,219.72	1,264.26	1,309.39	1,355.09	1,401.32	1,448.06
140,000.00	1,219.64	1,266.25	1,313.54	1,361.51	1,410.11	1,459.32	1,509.11	1,559.45
150,000.00	1,306.76	1,356.69	1,407.37	1,458.76	1,510.84	1,563.56	1,616.91	1,670.84
160,000.00	1,393.88	1,447.14	1,501.19	1,556.01	1,611.56	1,667.80	1,724.70	1,782.23
170,000.00	1,481.00	1,537.58	1,595.02	1,653.26	1,712.28	1,772.04	1,832.50	1,893.62
180,000.00	1,568.11	1,628.03	1,688.84	1,750.51	1,813.00	1,876.27	1,940.29	2,005.01
190,000.00	1,655.23	1,718.48	1,782.67	1,847.76	1,913.72	1,980.51	2,048.08	2,116.40
200,000.00	1,742.35	1,808.92	1,876.49	1,945.01	2,014.45	2,084.75	2,155.88	2,227.79
210,000.00	1,829.47	1,899.37	1,970.32	2,042.26	2,115.17	2,188.99	2,263.67	2,339.18
220,000.00	1,916.58	1,989.82	2,064.14	2,139.52	2,215.89	2,293.22	2,371.46	2,450.57
230,000.00	2,003.70	2,080.26	2,157.97	2,236.77	2,316.61	2,397.46	2,479.26	2,561.96
240,000.00	2,090.82	2,170.71	2,251.79	2,334.02	2,417.34	2,501.70	2,587.05	2,673.35
250,000.00	2,177.94	2,261.15	2,345.62	2,431.27	2,518.06	2,605.94	2,694.85	2,784.74
260,000.00	2,265.05	2,351.60	2,439.44	2,528.52	2,618.78	2,710.17	2,802.64	2,896.13
270,000.00	2,352.17	2,442.05	2,533.26	2,625.77	2,719.50	2,814.41	2,910.43	3,007.52
280,000.00	2,439.29	2,532.49	2,627.09	2,723.02	2,820.23	2,918.65	3,018.23	3,118.91
290,000.00	2,526.41	2,622.94	2,720.91	2,820.27	2,920.95	3,022.89	3,126.02	3,230.30

MORTGAGE COMPARISON

23 YEAR MORTGAGES

RATES -> AMOUNTS	5.000%	5.500%	6.000%	6.500%	7.000%	7.500%	8.000%	8.500%
50,000.00	305.20	319.64	334.42	349.53	364.96	380.69	396.73	413.04
60,000.00	366.24	383.57	401.31	419.44	437.95	456.83	476.07	495.65
70,000.00	427.28	447.50	468.19	489.35	510.94	532.97	555.42	578.26
80,000.00	488.32	511.43	535.08	559.25	583.94	609.11	634.76	660.87
90,000.00	549.37	575.36	601.96	629.16	656.93	685.25	714.11	743.48
100,000.00	610.41	639.29	668.85	699.06	729.92	761.39	793.45	826.09
110,000.00	671.45	703.22	735.73	768.97	802.91	837.53	872.80	908.70
120,000.00	732.49	767.15	802.62	838.88	875.90	913.67	952.14	991.30
130,000.00	793.53	831.07	869.50	908.78	948.90	989.81	1,031.49	1,073.91
140,000.00	854.57	895.00	936.39	978.69	1,021.89	1,065.95	1,110.83	1,156.52
150,000.00	915.61	958.93	1,003.27	1,048.60	1,094.88	1,142.08	1,190.18	1,239.13
160,000.00	976.65	1,022.86	1,070.16	1,118.50	1,167.87	1,218.22	1,269.52	1,321.74
170,000.00	1,037.69	1,086.79	1,137.04	1,188.41	1,240.86	1,294.36	1,348.87	1,404.35
180,000.00	1,098.73	1,150.72	1,203.93	1,258.32	1,313.85	1,370.50	1,428.21	1,486.96
190,000.00	1,159.77	1,214.65	1,270.81	1,328.22	1,386.85	1,446.64	1,507.56	1,569.56
200,000.00	1,220.81	1,278.58	1,337.69	1,398.13	1,459.84	1,522.78	1,586.91	1,652.17
210,000.00	1,281.85	1,342.50	1,404.58	1,468.04	1,532.83	1,598.92	1,666.25	1,734.78
220,000.00	1,342.89	1,406.43	1,471.46	1,537.94	1,605.82	1,675.06	1,745.60	1,817.39
230,000.00	1,403.93	1,470.36	1,538.35	1,607.85	1,678.81	1,751.20	1,824.94	1,900.00
240,000.00	1,464.97	1,534.29	1,605.23	1,677.76	1,751.81	1,827.33	1,904.29	1,982.61
250,000.00	1,526.02	1,598.22	1,672.12	1,747.66	1,824.80	1,903.47	1,983.63	2,065.22
260,000.00	1,587.06	1,662.15	1,739.00	1,817.57	1,897.79	1,979.61	2,062.98	2,147.83
270,000.00	1,648.10	1,726.08	1,805.89	1,887.47	1,970.78	2,055.75	2,142.32	2,230.43
280,000.00	1,709.14	1,790.01	1,872.77	1,957.38	2,043.77	2,131.89	2,221.67	2,313.04
290,000.00	1,770.18	1,853.93	1,939.66	2,027.29	2,116.77	2,208.03	2,301.01	2,395.65

RATES -> AMOUNTS	9.000%	9.500%	10.000%	10.500%	11.000%	11.500%	12.000%	12.500%
50,000.00	429.63	446.49	463.59	480.93	498.50	516.29	534.28	552.47
60,000.00	515.56	535.78	556.31	577.12	598.20	619.55	641.14	662.96
70,000.00	601.49	625.08	649.03	673.31	697.91	722.81	748.00	773.46
80,000.00	687.41	714.38	741.75	769.49	797.61	826.07	854.85	883.95
90,000.00	773.34	803.68	834.46	865.68	897.31	929.32	961.71	994.44
100,000.00	859.27	892.97	927.18	961.87	997.01	1,032.58	1,068.56	1,104.94
110,000.00	945.20	982.27	1,019.90	1,058.05	1,096.71	1,135.84	1,175.42	1,215.43
120,000.00	1,031.12	1,071.57	1,112.62	1,154.24	1,196.41	1,239.10	1,282.28	1,325.92
130,000.00	1,117.05	1,160.87	1,205.34	1,250.43	1,296.11	1,342.36	1,389.13	1,436.42
140,000.00	1,202.98	1,250.16	1,298.05	1,346.61	1,395.81	1,445.61	1,495.99	1,546.91
150,000.00	1,288.90	1,339.46	1,390.77	1,442.80	1,495.51	1,548.87	1,602.85	1,657.41
160,000.00	1,374.83	1,428.76	1,483.49	1,538.99	1,595.21	1,652.13	1,709.70	1,767.90
170,000.00	1,460.76	1,518.06	1,576.21	1,635.17	1,694.91	1,755.39	1,816.56	1,878.39
180,000.00	1,546.68	1,607.35	1,668.93	1,731.36	1,794.61	1,858.65	1,923.42	1,988.89
190,000.00	1,632.61	1,696.65	1,761.65	1,827.55	1,894.32	1,961.90	2,030.27	2,099.38
200,000.00	1,718.54	1,785.95	1,854.36	1,923.73	1,994.02	2,065.16	2,137.13	2,209.87
210,000.00	1,804.46	1,875.25	1,947.08	2,019.92	2,093.72	2,168.42	2,243.99	2,320.37
220,000.00	1,890.39	1,964.54	2,039.80	2,116.11	2,193.42	2,271.68	2,350.84	2,430.86
230,000.00	1,976.32	2,053.84	2,132.52	2,212.29	2,293.12	2,374.94	2,457.70	2,541.35
240,000.00	2,062.24	2,143.14	2,225.24	2,308.48	2,392.82	2,478.20	2,564.56	2,651.85
250,000.00	2,148.17	2,232.44	2,317.95	2,404.67	2,492.52	2,581.45	2,671.41	2,762.34
260,000.00	2,234.10	2,321.73	2,410.67	2,500.85	2,592.22	2,684.71	2,778.27	2,872.84
270,000.00	2,320.02	2,411.03	2,503.39	2,597.04	2,691.92	2,787.97	2,885.13	2,983.33
280,000.00	2,405.95	2,500.33	2,596.11	2,693.23	2,791.62	2,891.23	2,991.98	3,093.82
290,000.00	2,491.88	2,589.63	2,688.83	2,789.42	2,891.32	2,994.49	3,098.84	3,204.32

MORTGAGE COMPARISON
24 YEAR MORTGAGES

RATES -> AMOUNTS	5.000%	5.500%	6.000%	6.500%	7.000%	7.500%	8.000%	8.500%
50,000.00	298.45	313.04	327.99	343.27	358.88	374.80	391.03	407.54
60,000.00	358.14	375.65	393.59	411.93	430.66	449.76	469.23	489.05
70,000.00	417.83	438.26	459.18	480.58	502.43	524.72	547.44	570.56
80,000.00	477.52	500.87	524.78	549.23	574.21	599.68	625.64	652.07
90,000.00	537.21	563.48	590.38	617.89	645.98	674.64	703.85	733.57
100,000.00	596.90	626.09	655.98	686.54	717.76	749.61	782.05	815.08
110,000.00	656.59	688.70	721.58	755.20	789.54	824.57	860.26	896.59
120,000.00	716.28	751.31	787.17	823.85	861.31	899.53	938.47	978.10
130,000.00	775.97	813.92	852.77	892.51	933.09	974.49	1,016.67	1,059.61
140,000.00	835.66	876.52	918.37	961.16	1,004.86	1,049.45	1,094.88	1,141.12
150,000.00	895.35	939.13	983.97	1,029.81	1,076.64	1,124.41	1,173.08	1,222.62
160,000.00	955.04	1,001.74	1,049.56	1,098.47	1,148.42	1,199.37	1,251.29	1,304.13
170,000.00	1,014.73	1,064.35	1,115.16	1,167.12	1,220.19	1,274.33	1,329.49	1,385.64
180,000.00	1,074.42	1,126.96	1,180.76	1,235.78	1,291.97	1,349.29	1,407.70	1,467.15
190,000.00	1,134.11	1,189.57	1,246.36	1,304.43	1,363.74	1,424.25	1,485.90	1,548.66
200,000.00	1,193.80	1,252.18	1,311.96	1,373.09	1,435.52	1,499.21	1,564.11	1,630.16
210,000.00	1,253.48	1,314.79	1,377.55	1,441.74	1,507.30	1,574.17	1,642.31	1,711.67
220,000.00	1,313.17	1,377.40	1,443.15	1,510.39	1,579.07	1,649.13	1,720.52	1,793.18
230,000.00	1,372.86	1,440.00	1,508.75	1,579.05	1,650.85	1,724.09	1,798.72	1,874.69
240,000.00	1,432.55	1,502.61	1,574.35	1,647.70	1,722.62	1,799.05	1,876.93	1,956.20
250,000.00	1,492.24	1,565.22	1,639.95	1,716.36	1,794.40	1,874.01	1,955.14	2,037.71
260,000.00	1,551.93	1,627.83	1,705.54	1,785.01	1,866.18	1,948.97	2,033.34	2,119.21
270,000.00	1,611.62	1,690.44	1,771.14	1,853.67	1,937.95	2,023.93	2,111.55	2,200.72
280,000.00	1,671.31	1,753.05	1,836.74	1,922.32	2,009.73	2,098.89	2,189.75	2,282.23
290,000.00	1,731.00	1,815.66	1,902.34	1,990.97	2,081.50	2,173.85	2,267.96	2,363.74

RATES -> AMOUNTS	9.000%	9.500%	10.000%	10.500%	11.000%	11.500%	12.000%	12.500%
50,000.00	424.33	441.39	458.69	476.24	494.01	512.00	530.19	548.57
60,000.00	509.20	529.67	550.43	571.49	592.82	614.40	636.23	658.29
70,000.00	594.07	617.94	642.17	666.74	691.62	716.80	742.27	768.00
80,000.00	678.93	706.22	733.91	761.98	790.42	819.20	848.31	877.72
90,000.00	763.80	794.50	825.65	857.23	889.22	921.60	954.34	987.43
100,000.00	848.66	882.77	917.39	952.48	988.03	1,024.00	1,060.38	1,097.14
110,000.00	933.53	971.05	1,009.13	1,047.73	1,086.83	1,126.40	1,166.42	1,206.86
120,000.00	1,018.40	1,059.33	1,100.87	1,142.98	1,185.63	1,228.80	1,272.46	1,316.57
130,000.00	1,103.26	1,147.61	1,192.61	1,238.23	1,284.43	1,331.20	1,378.50	1,426.29
140,000.00	1,188.13	1,235.88	1,284.34	1,333.47	1,383.24	1,433.60	1,484.53	1,536.00
150,000.00	1,273.00	1,324.16	1,376.08	1,428.72	1,482.04	1,536.00	1,590.57	1,645.72
160,000.00	1,357.86	1,412.44	1,467.82	1,523.97	1,580.84	1,638.40	1,696.61	1,755.43
170,000.00	1,442.73	1,500.72	1,559.56	1,619.22	1,679.65	1,740.80	1,802.65	1,865.15
180,000.00	1,527.60	1,588.99	1,651.30	1,714.47	1,778.45	1,843.20	1,908.69	1,974.86
190,000.00	1,612.46	1,677.27	1,743.04	1,809.71	1,877.25	1,945.60	2,014.73	2,084.57
200,000.00	1,697.33	1,765.55	1,834.78	1,904.96	1,976.05	2,048.00	2,120.76	2,194.29
210,000.00	1,782.20	1,853.83	1,926.52	2,000.21	2,074.86	2,150.40	2,226.80	2,304.00
220,000.00	1,867.06	1,942.10	2,018.26	2,095.46	2,173.66	2,252.80	2,332.84	2,413.72
230,000.00	1,951.93	2,030.38	2,109.99	2,190.71	2,272.46	2,355.20	2,438.88	2,523.43
240,000.00	2,036.79	2,118.66	2,201.73	2,285.95	2,371.26	2,457.60	2,544.92	2,633.15
250,000.00	2,121.66	2,206.94	2,293.47	2,381.20	2,470.07	2,560.00	2,650.95	2,742.86
260,000.00	2,206.53	2,295.21	2,385.21	2,476.45	2,568.87	2,662.40	2,756.99	2,852.58
270,000.00	2,291.39	2,383.49	2,476.95	2,571.70	2,667.67	2,764.80	2,863.03	2,962.29
280,000.00	2,376.26	2,471.77	2,568.69	2,666.95	2,766.47	2,867.20	2,969.07	3,072.00
290,000.00	2,461.13	2,560.05	2,660.43	2,762.19	2,865.28	2,969.60	3,075.11	3,181.72

MORTGAGE COMPARISON

25 YEAR MORTGAGES

RATES -> AMOUNTS	5.000%	5.500%	6.000%	6.500%	7.000%	7.500%	8.000%	8.500%
50,000.00	292.30	307.04	322.15	337.60	353.39	369.50	385.91	402.61
60,000.00	350.75	368.45	386.58	405.12	424.07	443.39	463.09	483.14
70,000.00	409.21	429.86	451.01	472.65	494.75	517.29	540.27	563.66
80,000.00	467.67	491.27	515.44	540.17	565.42	591.19	617.45	644.18
90,000.00	526.13	552.68	579.87	607.69	636.10	665.09	694.63	724.70
100,000.00	584.59	614.09	644.30	675.21	706.78	738.99	771.82	805.23
110,000.00	643.05	675.50	708.73	742.73	777.46	812.89	849.00	885.75
120,000.00	701.51	736.91	773.16	810.25	848.14	886.79	926.18	966.27
130,000.00	759.97	798.31	837.59	877.77	918.81	960.69	1,003.36	1,046.80
140,000.00	818.43	859.72	902.02	945.29	989.49	1,034.59	1,080.54	1,127.32
150,000.00	876.89	921.13	966.45	1,012.81	1,060.17	1,108.49	1,157.72	1,207.84
160,000.00	935.34	982.54	1,030.88	1,080.33	1,130.85	1,182.39	1,234.91	1,288.36
170,000.00	993.80	1,043.95	1,095.31	1,147.85	1,201.52	1,256.29	1,312.09	1,368.89
180,000.00	1,052.26	1,105.36	1,159.74	1,215.37	1,272.20	1,330.18	1,389.27	1,449.41
190,000.00	1,110.72	1,166.77	1,224.17	1,282.89	1,342.88	1,404.08	1,466.45	1,529.93
200,000.00	1,169.18	1,228.18	1,288.60	1,350.41	1,413.56	1,477.98	1,543.63	1,610.45
210,000.00	1,227.64	1,289.58	1,353.03	1,417.94	1,484.24	1,551.88	1,620.81	1,690.98
220,000.00	1,286.10	1,350.99	1,417.46	1,485.46	1,554.91	1,625.78	1,698.00	1,771.50
230,000.00	1,344.56	1,412.40	1,481.89	1,552.98	1,625.59	1,699.68	1,775.18	1,852.02
240,000.00	1,403.02	1,473.81	1,546.32	1,620.50	1,696.27	1,773.58	1,852.36	1,932.55
250,000.00	1,461.48	1,535.22	1,610.75	1,688.02	1,766.95	1,847.48	1,929.54	2,013.07
260,000.00	1,519.93	1,596.63	1,675.18	1,755.54	1,837.63	1,921.38	2,006.72	2,093.59
270,000.00	1,578.39	1,658.04	1,739.61	1,823.06	1,908.30	1,995.28	2,083.90	2,174.11
280,000.00	1,636.85	1,719.45	1,804.04	1,890.58	1,978.98	2,069.18	2,161.09	2,254.64
290,000.00	1,695.31	1,780.85	1,868.47	1,958.10	2,049.66	2,143.07	2,238.27	2,335.16

RATES -> AMOUNTS	9.000%	9.500%	10.000%	10.500%	11.000%	11.500%	12.000%	12.500%
50,000.00	419.60	436.85	454.35	472.09	490.06	508.23	526.61	545.18
60,000.00	503.52	524.22	545.22	566.51	588.07	609.88	631.93	654.21
70,000.00	587.44	611.59	636.09	660.93	686.08	711.53	737.26	763.25
80,000.00	671.36	698.96	726.96	755.35	784.09	813.18	842.58	872.28
90,000.00	755.28	786.33	817.83	849.76	882.10	914.82	947.90	981.32
100,000.00	839.20	873.70	908.70	944.18	980.11	1,016.47	1,053.22	1,090.35
110,000.00	923.12	961.07	999.57	1,038.60	1,078.12	1,118.12	1,158.55	1,199.39
120,000.00	1,007.04	1,048.44	1,090.44	1,133.02	1,176.14	1,219.76	1,263.87	1,308.43
130,000.00	1,090.96	1,135.81	1,181.31	1,227.44	1,274.15	1,321.41	1,369.19	1,417.46
140,000.00	1,174.87	1,223.18	1,272.18	1,321.85	1,372.16	1,423.06	1,474.51	1,526.50
150,000.00	1,258.79	1,310.55	1,363.05	1,416.27	1,470.17	1,524.70	1,579.84	1,635.53
160,000.00	1,342.71	1,397.91	1,453.92	1,510.69	1,568.18	1,626.35	1,685.16	1,744.57
170,000.00	1,426.63	1,485.28	1,544.79	1,605.11	1,666.19	1,728.00	1,790.48	1,853.60
180,000.00	1,510.55	1,572.65	1,635.66	1,699.53	1,764.20	1,829.64	1,895.80	1,962.64
190,000.00	1,594.47	1,660.02	1,726.53	1,793.95	1,862.21	1,931.29	2,001.13	2,071.67
200,000.00	1,678.39	1,747.39	1,817.40	1,888.36	1,960.23	2,032.94	2,106.45	2,180.71
210,000.00	1,762.31	1,834.76	1,908.27	1,982.78	2,058.24	2,134.58	2,211.77	2,289.74
220,000.00	1,846.23	1,922.13	1,999.14	2,077.20	2,156.25	2,236.23	2,317.09	2,398.78
230,000.00	1,930.15	2,009.50	2,090.01	2,171.62	2,254.26	2,337.88	2,422.42	2,507.81
240,000.00	2,014.07	2,096.87	2,180.88	2,266.04	2,352.27	2,439.53	2,527.74	2,616.85
250,000.00	2,097.99	2,184.24	2,271.75	2,360.45	2,450.28	2,541.17	2,633.06	2,725.89
260,000.00	2,181.91	2,271.61	2,362.62	2,454.87	2,548.29	2,642.82	2,738.38	2,834.92
270,000.00	2,265.83	2,358.98	2,453.49	2,549.29	2,646.31	2,744.47	2,843.71	2,943.96
280,000.00	2,349.75	2,446.35	2,544.36	2,643.71	2,744.32	2,846.11	2,949.03	3,052.99
290,000.00	2,433.67	2,533.72	2,635.23	2,738.13	2,842.33	2,947.76	3,054.35	3,162.03

MORTGAGE COMPARISON
26 YEAR MORTGAGES

RATES -> AMOUNTS	5.000%	5.500%	6.000%	6.500%	7.000%	7.500%	8.000%	8.500%
50,000.00	286.67	301.57	316.84	332.46	348.42	364.70	381.30	398.19
60,000.00	344.01	361.89	380.21	398.95	418.10	437.64	457.56	477.83
70,000.00	401.34	422.20	443.57	465.44	487.79	510.59	533.82	557.47
80,000.00	458.68	482.51	506.94	531.93	557.47	583.53	610.08	637.10
90,000.00	516.01	542.83	570.31	598.43	627.15	656.47	686.34	716.74
100,000.00	573.34	603.14	633.68	664.92	696.84	729.41	762.60	796.38
110,000.00	630.68	663.46	697.04	731.41	766.52	802.35	838.86	876.02
120,000.00	688.01	723.77	760.41	797.90	836.21	875.29	915.12	955.66
130,000.00	745.35	784.09	823.78	864.39	905.89	948.23	991.38	1,035.29
140,000.00	802.68	844.40	887.15	930.89	975.57	1,021.17	1,067.64	1,114.93
150,000.00	860.02	904.71	950.52	997.38	1,045.26	1,094.11	1,143.90	1,194.57
160,000.00	917.35	965.03	1,013.88	1,063.87	1,114.94	1,167.05	1,220.16	1,274.21
170,000.00	974.68	1,025.34	1,077.25	1,130.36	1,184.62	1,239.99	1,296.42	1,353.85
180,000.00	1,032.02	1,085.66	1,140.62	1,196.85	1,254.31	1,312.93	1,372.68	1,433.48
190,000.00	1,089.35	1,145.97	1,203.99	1,263.34	1,323.99	1,385.87	1,448.94	1,513.12
200,000.00	1,146.69	1,206.29	1,267.35	1,329.84	1,393.68	1,458.81	1,525.20	1,592.76
210,000.00	1,204.02	1,266.60	1,330.72	1,396.33	1,463.36	1,531.76	1,601.46	1,672.40
220,000.00	1,261.36	1,326.92	1,394.09	1,462.82	1,533.04	1,604.70	1,677.72	1,752.04
230,000.00	1,318.69	1,387.23	1,457.46	1,529.31	1,602.73	1,677.64	1,753.98	1,831.67
240,000.00	1,376.02	1,447.54	1,520.82	1,595.80	1,672.41	1,750.58	1,830.24	1,911.31
250,000.00	1,433.36	1,507.86	1,584.19	1,662.29	1,742.09	1,823.52	1,906.50	1,990.95
260,000.00	1,490.69	1,568.17	1,647.56	1,728.79	1,811.78	1,896.46	1,982.76	2,070.59
270,000.00	1,548.03	1,628.49	1,710.93	1,795.28	1,881.46	1,969.40	2,059.02	2,150.23
280,000.00	1,605.36	1,688.80	1,774.30	1,861.77	1,951.15	2,042.34	2,135.27	2,229.86
290,000.00	1,662.70	1,749.12	1,837.66	1,928.26	2,020.83	2,115.28	2,211.53	2,309.50

RATES -> AMOUNTS	9.000%	9.500%	10.000%	10.500%	11.000%	11.500%	12.000%	12.500%
50,000.00	415.36	432.80	450.49	468.41	486.56	504.92	523.48	542.21
60,000.00	498.43	519.36	540.59	562.10	583.88	605.91	628.17	650.66
70,000.00	581.51	605.92	630.68	655.78	681.19	706.89	732.87	759.10
80,000.00	664.58	692.48	720.78	749.46	778.50	807.88	837.56	867.54
90,000.00	747.65	779.04	810.88	843.15	875.81	908.86	942.26	975.98
100,000.00	830.72	865.60	900.98	936.83	973.13	1,009.84	1,046.95	1,084.43
110,000.00	913.80	952.16	991.07	1,030.51	1,070.44	1,110.83	1,151.65	1,192.87
120,000.00	996.87	1,038.72	1,081.17	1,124.20	1,167.75	1,211.81	1,256.34	1,301.31
130,000.00	1,079.94	1,125.28	1,171.27	1,217.88	1,265.07	1,312.80	1,361.04	1,409.76
140,000.00	1,163.01	1,211.84	1,261.37	1,311.56	1,362.38	1,413.78	1,465.73	1,518.20
150,000.00	1,246.09	1,298.40	1,351.47	1,405.24	1,459.69	1,514.77	1,570.43	1,626.64
160,000.00	1,329.16	1,384.96	1,441.56	1,498.93	1,557.00	1,615.75	1,675.12	1,735.08
170,000.00	1,412.23	1,471.52	1,531.66	1,592.61	1,654.32	1,716.73	1,779.82	1,843.53
180,000.00	1,495.30	1,558.08	1,621.76	1,686.29	1,751.63	1,817.72	1,884.51	1,951.97
190,000.00	1,578.37	1,644.64	1,711.86	1,779.98	1,848.94	1,918.70	1,989.21	2,060.41
200,000.00	1,661.45	1,731.20	1,801.96	1,873.66	1,946.25	2,019.69	2,093.90	2,168.85
210,000.00	1,744.52	1,817.76	1,892.05	1,967.34	2,043.57	2,120.67	2,198.60	2,277.30
220,000.00	1,827.59	1,904.32	1,982.15	2,061.02	2,140.88	2,221.66	2,303.30	2,385.74
230,000.00	1,910.66	1,990.88	2,072.25	2,154.71	2,238.19	2,322.64	2,407.99	2,494.18
240,000.00	1,993.74	2,077.44	2,162.34	2,248.39	2,335.51	2,423.63	2,512.69	2,602.63
250,000.00	2,076.81	2,164.00	2,252.44	2,342.07	2,432.82	2,524.61	2,617.38	2,711.07
260,000.00	2,159.88	2,250.56	2,342.54	2,435.76	2,530.13	2,625.59	2,722.08	2,819.51
270,000.00	2,242.95	2,337.12	2,432.64	2,529.44	2,627.44	2,726.58	2,826.77	2,927.95
280,000.00	2,326.03	2,423.68	2,522.74	2,623.12	2,724.76	2,827.56	2,931.47	3,036.40
290,000.00	2,409.10	2,510.24	2,612.83	2,716.80	2,822.07	2,928.55	3,036.16	3,144.84

MORTGAGE COMPARISON

27 YEAR MORTGAGES

RATES -> AMOUNTS	5.000%	5.500%	6.000%	6.500%	7.000%	7.500%	8.000%	8.500%
50,000.00	281.52	296.57	311.99	327.78	343.91	360.37	377.14	394.21
60,000.00	337.82	355.88	374.39	393.33	412.69	432.44	452.57	473.05
70,000.00	394.13	415.20	436.79	458.89	481.47	504.51	528.00	551.89
80,000.00	450.43	474.51	499.19	524.44	550.25	576.59	603.42	630.74
90,000.00	506.74	533.82	561.59	590.00	619.03	648.66	678.85	709.58
100,000.00	563.04	593.14	623.99	655.56	687.82	720.73	754.28	788.42
110,000.00	619.34	652.45	686.38	721.11	756.60	792.81	829.71	867.26
120,000.00	675.65	711.76	748.78	786.67	825.38	864.88	905.14	946.11
130,000.00	731.95	771.08	811.18	852.22	894.16	936.95	980.56	1,024.95
140,000.00	788.25	830.39	873.58	917.78	962.94	1,009.03	1,055.99	1,103.79
150,000.00	844.56	889.71	935.98	983.33	1,031.72	1,081.10	1,131.42	1,182.63
160,000.00	900.86	949.02	998.38	1,048.89	1,100.50	1,153.17	1,206.85	1,261.47
170,000.00	957.17	1,008.33	1,060.78	1,114.44	1,169.29	1,225.25	1,282.28	1,340.32
180,000.00	1,013.47	1,067.65	1,123.17	1,180.00	1,238.07	1,297.32	1,357.70	1,419.16
190,000.00	1,069.77	1,126.96	1,185.57	1,245.55	1,306.85	1,369.39	1,433.13	1,498.00
200,000.00	1,126.08	1,186.27	1,247.97	1,311.11	1,375.63	1,441.47	1,508.56	1,576.84
210,000.00	1,182.38	1,245.59	1,310.37	1,376.67	1,444.41	1,513.54	1,583.99	1,655.68
220,000.00	1,238.69	1,304.90	1,372.77	1,442.22	1,513.19	1,585.61	1,659.42	1,734.53
230,000.00	1,294.99	1,364.21	1,435.17	1,507.78	1,581.97	1,657.69	1,734.84	1,813.37
240,000.00	1,351.29	1,423.53	1,497.56	1,573.33	1,650.76	1,729.76	1,810.27	1,892.21
250,000.00	1,407.60	1,482.84	1,559.96	1,638.89	1,719.54	1,801.83	1,885.70	1,971.05
260,000.00	1,463.90	1,542.16	1,622.36	1,704.44	1,788.32	1,873.91	1,961.13	2,049.89
270,000.00	1,520.21	1,601.47	1,684.76	1,770.00	1,857.10	1,945.98	2,036.56	2,128.74
280,000.00	1,576.51	1,660.78	1,747.16	1,835.55	1,925.88	2,018.05	2,111.98	2,207.58
290,000.00	1,632.81	1,720.10	1,809.56	1,901.11	1,994.66	2,090.13	2,187.41	2,286.42

RATES -> AMOUNTS	9.000%	9.500%	10.000%	10.500%	11.000%	11.500%	12.000%	12.500%
50,000.00	411.56	429.18	447.05	465.15	483.48	502.00	520.72	539.62
60,000.00	493.88	515.02	536.46	558.18	580.17	602.40	624.87	647.55
70,000.00	576.19	600.85	625.87	651.21	676.87	702.81	729.01	755.47
80,000.00	658.50	686.69	715.28	744.24	773.56	803.21	833.16	863.40
90,000.00	740.81	772.53	804.69	837.27	870.26	903.61	937.30	971.32
100,000.00	823.13	858.36	894.10	930.30	966.95	1,004.01	1,041.45	1,079.25
110,000.00	905.44	944.20	983.51	1,023.33	1,063.65	1,104.41	1,145.59	1,187.17
120,000.00	987.75	1,030.03	1,072.92	1,116.36	1,160.34	1,204.81	1,249.74	1,295.10
130,000.00	1,070.06	1,115.87	1,162.33	1,209.40	1,257.04	1,305.21	1,353.88	1,403.02
140,000.00	1,152.38	1,201.71	1,251.74	1,302.43	1,353.73	1,405.61	1,458.03	1,510.95
150,000.00	1,234.69	1,287.54	1,341.15	1,395.46	1,450.43	1,506.01	1,562.17	1,618.87
160,000.00	1,317.00	1,373.38	1,430.56	1,488.49	1,547.12	1,606.41	1,666.32	1,726.80
170,000.00	1,399.31	1,459.21	1,519.97	1,581.52	1,643.82	1,706.81	1,770.46	1,834.72
180,000.00	1,481.63	1,545.05	1,609.38	1,674.55	1,740.51	1,807.21	1,874.61	1,942.64
190,000.00	1,563.94	1,630.89	1,698.79	1,767.58	1,837.21	1,907.61	1,978.75	2,050.57
200,000.00	1,646.25	1,716.72	1,788.20	1,860.61	1,933.90	2,008.02	2,082.90	2,158.49
210,000.00	1,728.56	1,802.56	1,877.61	1,953.64	2,030.60	2,108.42	2,187.04	2,266.42
220,000.00	1,810.88	1,888.40	1,967.02	2,046.67	2,127.29	2,208.82	2,291.19	2,374.34
230,000.00	1,893.19	1,974.23	2,056.42	2,139.70	2,223.99	2,309.22	2,395.33	2,482.27
240,000.00	1,975.50	2,060.07	2,145.83	2,232.73	2,320.68	2,409.62	2,499.48	2,590.19
250,000.00	2,057.81	2,145.90	2,235.24	2,325.76	2,417.38	2,510.02	2,603.62	2,698.12
260,000.00	2,140.13	2,231.74	2,324.65	2,418.79	2,514.07	2,610.42	2,707.77	2,806.04
270,000.00	2,222.44	2,317.58	2,414.06	2,511.82	2,610.77	2,710.82	2,811.91	2,913.97
280,000.00	2,304.75	2,403.41	2,503.47	2,604.85	2,707.46	2,811.22	2,916.06	3,021.89
290,000.00	2,387.06	2,489.25	2,592.88	2,697.88	2,804.16	2,911.62	3,020.20	3,129.82

MORTGAGE COMPARISON

28 YEAR MORTGAGES

RATES ->	5.000%	5.500%	6.000%	6.500%	7.000%	7.500%	8.000%	8.500%
AMOUNTS								
50,000.00	276.79	291.98	307.56	323.51	339.80	356.43	373.38	390.62
60,000.00	332.14	350.38	369.07	388.21	407.77	427.72	448.06	468.75
70,000.00	387.50	408.78	430.59	452.91	475.73	499.01	522.73	546.87
80,000.00	442.86	467.17	492.10	517.61	543.69	570.29	597.41	625.00
90,000.00	498.22	525.57	553.61	582.31	611.65	641.58	672.08	703.12
100,000.00	553.57	583.97	615.12	647.02	679.61	712.87	746.76	781.25
110,000.00	608.93	642.36	676.64	711.72	747.57	784.15	821.43	859.37
120,000.00	664.29	700.76	738.15	776.42	815.53	855.44	896.11	937.50
130,000.00	719.65	759.16	799.66	841.12	883.49	926.73	970.79	1,015.62
140,000.00	775.00	817.55	861.17	905.82	951.45	998.01	1,045.46	1,093.75
150,000.00	830.36	875.95	922.69	970.52	1,019.41	1,069.30	1,120.14	1,171.87
160,000.00	885.72	934.35	984.20	1,035.23	1,087.37	1,140.59	1,194.81	1,250.00
170,000.00	941.08	992.74	1,045.71	1,099.93	1,155.33	1,211.88	1,269.49	1,328.12
180,000.00	996.43	1,051.14	1,107.22	1,164.63	1,223.30	1,283.16	1,344.17	1,406.25
190,000.00	1,051.79	1,109.54	1,168.74	1,229.33	1,291.26	1,354.45	1,418.84	1,484.37
200,000.00	1,107.15	1,167.93	1,230.25	1,294.03	1,359.22	1,425.74	1,493.52	1,562.49
210,000.00	1,162.51	1,226.33	1,291.76	1,358.73	1,427.18	1,497.02	1,568.19	1,640.62
220,000.00	1,217.86	1,284.72	1,353.27	1,423.44	1,495.14	1,568.31	1,642.87	1,718.74
230,000.00	1,273.22	1,343.12	1,414.79	1,488.14	1,563.10	1,639.60	1,717.55	1,796.87
240,000.00	1,328.58	1,401.52	1,476.30	1,552.84	1,631.06	1,710.88	1,792.22	1,874.99
250,000.00	1,383.94	1,459.91	1,537.81	1,617.54	1,699.02	1,782.17	1,866.90	1,953.12
260,000.00	1,439.29	1,518.31	1,599.32	1,682.24	1,766.98	1,853.46	1,941.57	2,031.24
270,000.00	1,494.65	1,576.71	1,660.83	1,746.94	1,834.94	1,924.74	2,016.25	2,109.37
280,000.00	1,550.01	1,635.10	1,722.35	1,811.65	1,902.90	1,996.03	2,090.92	2,187.49
290,000.00	1,605.36	1,693.50	1,783.86	1,876.35	1,970.87	2,067.32	2,165.60	2,265.62

RATES ->	9.000%	9.500%	10.000%	10.500%	11.000%	11.500%	12.000%	12.500%
AMOUNTS								
50,000.00	408.15	425.94	443.98	462.25	480.74	499.43	518.31	537.36
60,000.00	489.78	511.13	532.78	554.70	576.89	599.32	621.97	644.83
70,000.00	571.41	596.32	621.57	647.15	673.04	699.20	725.63	752.30
80,000.00	653.04	681.51	710.37	739.60	769.18	799.09	829.29	859.77
90,000.00	734.67	766.69	799.16	832.05	865.33	898.97	932.95	967.24
100,000.00	816.30	851.88	887.96	924.50	961.48	998.86	1,036.61	1,074.71
110,000.00	897.93	937.07	976.76	1,016.95	1,057.63	1,098.75	1,140.27	1,182.18
120,000.00	979.56	1,022.26	1,065.55	1,109.40	1,153.78	1,198.63	1,243.94	1,289.66
130,000.00	1,061.19	1,107.45	1,154.35	1,201.85	1,249.92	1,298.52	1,347.60	1,397.13
140,000.00	1,142.82	1,192.63	1,243.14	1,294.31	1,346.07	1,398.40	1,451.26	1,504.60
150,000.00	1,224.45	1,277.82	1,331.94	1,386.76	1,442.22	1,498.29	1,554.92	1,612.07
160,000.00	1,306.08	1,363.01	1,420.74	1,479.21	1,538.37	1,598.18	1,658.58	1,719.54
170,000.00	1,387.71	1,448.20	1,509.53	1,571.66	1,634.52	1,698.06	1,762.24	1,827.01
180,000.00	1,469.34	1,533.39	1,598.33	1,664.11	1,730.66	1,797.95	1,865.90	1,934.48
190,000.00	1,550.97	1,618.58	1,687.12	1,756.56	1,826.81	1,897.83	1,969.56	2,041.95
200,000.00	1,632.60	1,703.76	1,775.92	1,849.01	1,922.96	1,997.72	2,073.23	2,149.43
210,000.00	1,714.23	1,788.95	1,864.72	1,941.46	2,019.11	2,097.60	2,176.89	2,256.90
220,000.00	1,795.86	1,874.14	1,953.51	2,033.91	2,115.26	2,197.49	2,280.55	2,364.37
230,000.00	1,877.49	1,959.33	2,042.31	2,126.36	2,211.40	2,297.38	2,384.21	2,471.84
240,000.00	1,959.12	2,044.52	2,131.11	2,218.81	2,307.55	2,397.26	2,487.87	2,579.31
250,000.00	2,040.75	2,129.70	2,219.90	2,311.26	2,403.70	2,497.15	2,591.53	2,686.78
260,000.00	2,122.38	2,214.89	2,308.70	2,403.71	2,499.85	2,597.03	2,695.19	2,794.25
270,000.00	2,204.01	2,300.08	2,397.49	2,496.16	2,596.00	2,696.92	2,798.86	2,901.73
280,000.00	2,285.64	2,385.27	2,486.29	2,588.61	2,692.14	2,796.81	2,902.52	3,009.20
290,000.00	2,367.27	2,470.46	2,575.09	2,681.06	2,788.29	2,896.69	3,006.18	3,116.67

MORTGAGE COMPARISON
29 YEAR MORTGAGES

RATES -> AMOUNTS	5.000%	5.500%	6.000%	6.500%	7.000%	7.500%	8.000%	8.500%
50,000.00	272.43	287.77	303.50	319.61	336.07	352.86	369.97	387.39
60,000.00	326.92	345.33	364.20	383.53	403.28	423.43	443.97	464.86
70,000.00	381.40	402.88	424.90	447.45	470.49	494.00	517.96	542.34
80,000.00	435.89	460.43	485.60	511.37	537.70	564.58	591.96	619.82
90,000.00	490.37	517.99	546.30	575.29	604.92	635.15	665.95	697.29
100,000.00	544.86	575.54	607.00	639.21	672.13	705.72	739.95	774.77
110,000.00	599.35	633.10	667.71	703.13	739.34	776.29	813.94	852.25
120,000.00	653.83	690.65	728.41	767.06	806.56	846.86	887.94	929.72
130,000.00	708.32	748.20	789.11	830.98	873.77	917.44	961.93	1,007.20
140,000.00	762.80	805.76	849.81	894.90	940.98	988.01	1,035.92	1,084.68
150,000.00	817.29	863.31	910.51	958.82	1,008.20	1,058.58	1,109.92	1,162.16
160,000.00	871.78	920.87	971.21	1,022.74	1,075.41	1,129.15	1,183.91	1,239.63
170,000.00	926.26	978.42	1,031.91	1,086.66	1,142.62	1,199.72	1,257.91	1,317.11
180,000.00	980.75	1,035.98	1,092.61	1,150.58	1,209.83	1,270.30	1,331.90	1,394.59
190,000.00	1,035.23	1,093.53	1,153.31	1,214.50	1,277.05	1,340.87	1,405.90	1,472.06
200,000.00	1,089.72	1,151.08	1,214.01	1,278.43	1,344.26	1,411.44	1,479.89	1,549.54
210,000.00	1,144.21	1,208.64	1,274.71	1,342.35	1,411.47	1,482.01	1,553.89	1,627.02
220,000.00	1,198.69	1,266.19	1,335.41	1,406.27	1,478.69	1,552.58	1,627.88	1,704.50
230,000.00	1,253.18	1,323.75	1,396.11	1,470.19	1,545.90	1,623.16	1,701.88	1,781.97
240,000.00	1,307.66	1,381.30	1,456.81	1,534.11	1,613.11	1,693.73	1,775.87	1,859.45
250,000.00	1,362.15	1,438.86	1,517.51	1,598.03	1,680.33	1,764.30	1,849.86	1,936.93
260,000.00	1,416.64	1,496.41	1,578.21	1,661.95	1,747.54	1,834.87	1,923.86	2,014.40
270,000.00	1,471.12	1,553.96	1,638.91	1,725.87	1,814.75	1,905.44	1,997.85	2,091.88
280,000.00	1,525.61	1,611.52	1,699.61	1,789.80	1,881.96	1,976.02	2,071.85	2,169.36
290,000.00	1,580.10	1,669.07	1,760.31	1,853.72	1,949.18	2,046.59	2,145.84	2,246.83

RATES -> AMOUNTS	9.000%	9.500%	10.000%	10.500%	11.000%	11.500%	12.000%	12.500%
50,000.00	405.08	423.04	441.24	459.67	478.31	497.16	516.18	535.37
60,000.00	486.09	507.64	529.49	551.60	573.98	596.59	619.42	642.44
70,000.00	567.11	592.25	617.73	643.54	669.64	696.02	722.65	749.52
80,000.00	648.13	676.86	705.98	735.47	765.30	795.45	825.89	856.59
90,000.00	729.14	761.46	794.23	827.41	860.97	894.88	929.12	963.67
100,000.00	810.16	846.07	882.48	919.34	956.63	994.31	1,032.36	1,070.74
110,000.00	891.17	930.68	970.72	1,011.27	1,052.29	1,093.74	1,135.59	1,177.82
120,000.00	972.19	1,015.29	1,058.97	1,103.21	1,147.96	1,193.17	1,238.83	1,284.89
130,000.00	1,053.20	1,099.89	1,147.22	1,195.14	1,243.62	1,292.61	1,342.07	1,391.96
140,000.00	1,134.22	1,184.50	1,235.47	1,287.08	1,339.28	1,392.04	1,445.30	1,499.04
150,000.00	1,215.24	1,269.11	1,323.72	1,379.01	1,434.94	1,491.47	1,548.54	1,606.11
160,000.00	1,296.25	1,353.71	1,411.96	1,470.95	1,530.61	1,590.90	1,651.77	1,713.19
170,000.00	1,377.27	1,438.32	1,500.21	1,562.88	1,626.27	1,690.33	1,755.01	1,820.26
180,000.00	1,458.28	1,522.93	1,588.46	1,654.81	1,721.93	1,789.76	1,858.25	1,927.33
190,000.00	1,539.30	1,607.54	1,676.71	1,746.75	1,817.60	1,889.19	1,961.48	2,034.41
200,000.00	1,620.32	1,692.14	1,764.95	1,838.68	1,913.26	1,988.62	2,064.72	2,141.48
210,000.00	1,701.33	1,776.75	1,853.20	1,930.62	2,008.92	2,088.06	2,167.95	2,248.56
220,000.00	1,782.35	1,861.36	1,941.45	2,022.55	2,104.58	2,187.49	2,271.19	2,355.63
230,000.00	1,863.36	1,945.96	2,029.70	2,114.48	2,200.25	2,286.92	2,374.43	2,462.70
240,000.00	1,944.38	2,030.57	2,117.95	2,206.42	2,295.91	2,386.35	2,477.66	2,569.78
250,000.00	2,025.39	2,115.18	2,206.19	2,298.35	2,391.57	2,485.78	2,580.90	2,676.85
260,000.00	2,106.41	2,199.79	2,294.44	2,390.29	2,487.24	2,585.21	2,684.13	2,783.93
270,000.00	2,187.43	2,284.39	2,382.69	2,482.22	2,582.90	2,684.64	2,787.37	2,891.00
280,000.00	2,268.44	2,369.00	2,470.94	2,574.15	2,678.56	2,784.07	2,890.60	2,998.08
290,000.00	2,349.46	2,453.61	2,559.18	2,666.09	2,774.23	2,883.51	2,993.84	3,105.15

MORTGAGE COMPARISON
30 YEAR MORTGAGES

RATES -> AMOUNTS	5.000%	5.500%	6.000%	6.500%	7.000%	7.500%	8.000%	8.500%
50,000.00	268.41	283.89	299.78	316.03	332.65	349.61	366.88	384.46
60,000.00	322.09	340.67	359.73	379.24	399.18	419.53	440.26	461.35
70,000.00	375.78	397.45	419.69	442.45	465.71	489.45	513.64	538.24
80,000.00	429.46	454.23	479.64	505.65	532.24	559.37	587.01	615.13
90,000.00	483.14	511.01	539.60	568.86	598.77	629.29	660.39	692.02
100,000.00	536.82	567.79	599.55	632.07	665.30	699.21	733.76	768.91
110,000.00	590.50	624.57	659.51	695.27	731.83	769.14	807.14	845.80
120,000.00	644.19	681.35	719.46	758.48	798.36	839.06	880.52	922.70
130,000.00	697.87	738.13	779.42	821.69	864.89	908.98	953.89	999.59
140,000.00	751.55	794.90	839.37	884.90	931.42	978.90	1,027.27	1,076.48
150,000.00	805.23	851.68	899.33	948.10	997.95	1,048.82	1,100.65	1,153.37
160,000.00	858.91	908.46	959.28	1,011.31	1,064.48	1,118.74	1,174.02	1,230.26
170,000.00	912.60	965.24	1,019.24	1,074.52	1,131.01	1,188.66	1,247.40	1,307.15
180,000.00	966.28	1,022.02	1,079.19	1,137.72	1,197.54	1,258.59	1,320.78	1,384.04
190,000.00	1,019.96	1,078.80	1,139.15	1,200.93	1,264.07	1,328.51	1,394.15	1,460.94
200,000.00	1,073.64	1,135.58	1,199.10	1,264.14	1,330.61	1,398.43	1,467.53	1,537.83
210,000.00	1,127.33	1,192.36	1,259.06	1,327.34	1,397.14	1,468.35	1,540.91	1,614.72
220,000.00	1,181.01	1,249.14	1,319.01	1,390.55	1,463.67	1,538.27	1,614.28	1,691.61
230,000.00	1,234.69	1,305.91	1,378.97	1,453.76	1,530.20	1,608.19	1,687.66	1,768.50
240,000.00	1,288.37	1,362.69	1,438.92	1,516.96	1,596.73	1,678.11	1,761.04	1,845.39
250,000.00	1,342.05	1,419.47	1,498.88	1,580.17	1,663.26	1,748.04	1,834.41	1,922.28
260,000.00	1,395.74	1,476.25	1,558.83	1,643.38	1,729.79	1,817.96	1,907.79	1,999.18
270,000.00	1,449.42	1,533.03	1,618.79	1,706.58	1,796.32	1,887.88	1,981.16	2,076.07
280,000.00	1,503.10	1,589.81	1,678.74	1,769.79	1,862.85	1,957.80	2,054.54	2,152.96
290,000.00	1,556.78	1,646.59	1,738.70	1,833.00	1,929.38	2,027.72	2,127.92	2,229.85

RATES -> AMOUNTS	9.000%	9.500%	10.000%	10.500%	11.000%	11.500%	12.000%	12.500%
50,000.00	402.31	420.43	438.79	457.37	476.16	495.15	514.31	533.63
60,000.00	482.77	504.51	526.54	548.84	571.39	594.17	617.17	640.35
70,000.00	563.24	588.60	614.30	640.32	666.63	693.20	720.03	747.08
80,000.00	643.70	672.68	702.06	731.79	761.86	792.23	822.89	853.81
90,000.00	724.16	756.77	789.81	823.27	857.09	891.26	925.75	960.53
100,000.00	804.62	840.85	877.57	914.74	952.32	990.29	1,028.61	1,067.26
110,000.00	885.08	924.94	965.33	1,006.21	1,047.56	1,089.32	1,131.47	1,173.98
120,000.00	965.55	1,009.03	1,053.09	1,097.69	1,142.79	1,188.35	1,234.34	1,280.71
130,000.00	1,046.01	1,093.11	1,140.84	1,189.16	1,238.02	1,287.38	1,337.20	1,387.44
140,000.00	1,126.47	1,177.20	1,228.60	1,280.64	1,333.25	1,386.41	1,440.06	1,494.16
150,000.00	1,206.93	1,261.28	1,316.36	1,372.11	1,428.49	1,485.44	1,542.92	1,600.89
160,000.00	1,287.40	1,345.37	1,404.11	1,463.58	1,523.72	1,584.47	1,645.78	1,707.61
170,000.00	1,367.86	1,429.45	1,491.87	1,555.06	1,618.95	1,683.50	1,748.64	1,814.34
180,000.00	1,448.32	1,513.54	1,579.63	1,646.53	1,714.18	1,782.52	1,851.50	1,921.06
190,000.00	1,528.78	1,597.62	1,667.39	1,738.00	1,809.41	1,881.55	1,954.36	2,027.79
200,000.00	1,609.25	1,681.71	1,755.14	1,829.48	1,904.65	1,980.58	2,057.23	2,134.52
210,000.00	1,689.71	1,765.79	1,842.90	1,920.95	1,999.88	2,079.61	2,160.09	2,241.24
220,000.00	1,770.17	1,849.88	1,930.66	2,012.43	2,095.11	2,178.64	2,262.95	2,347.97
230,000.00	1,850.63	1,933.96	2,018.41	2,103.90	2,190.34	2,277.67	2,365.81	2,454.69
240,000.00	1,931.09	2,018.05	2,106.17	2,195.37	2,285.58	2,376.70	2,468.67	2,561.42
250,000.00	2,011.56	2,102.14	2,193.93	2,286.85	2,380.81	2,475.73	2,571.53	2,668.14
260,000.00	2,092.02	2,186.22	2,281.69	2,378.32	2,476.04	2,574.76	2,674.39	2,774.87
270,000.00	2,172.48	2,270.31	2,369.44	2,469.80	2,571.27	2,673.79	2,777.25	2,881.60
280,000.00	2,252.94	2,354.39	2,457.20	2,561.27	2,666.51	2,772.82	2,880.12	2,988.32
290,000.00	2,333.41	2,438.48	2,544.96	2,652.74	2,761.74	2,871.85	2,982.98	3,095.05

Appendix F
Worksheets

Walls:

	Room	Room	Room
Out of square	_____	_____	_____
Corners don't meet	_____	_____	_____
Drywall seams show	_____	_____	_____
Trim broken/missing	_____	_____	_____
Gouges in surface	_____	_____	_____
Registers not flush	_____	_____	_____
Wallcovering bubbled	_____	_____	_____
Ripped/wrong	_____	_____	_____
Nails/screws not set	_____	_____	_____
Corner bead dented	_____	_____	_____
Wrong paint/color	_____	_____	_____
Plaster stained	_____	_____	_____
Cracked/flaking	_____	_____	_____
_____	_____	_____	_____
_____	_____	_____	_____
_____	_____	_____	_____

Comments: _____

_____

_____

_____

_____

Floors:

	Room	Room	Room
Floors bowed/out of/	_____	_____	_____
square/squeak/crack	_____	_____	_____
Coverings ripped/loose/	_____	_____	_____
discolored/wrong	_____	_____	_____
Cove base missing	_____	_____	_____
Wrong color/type	_____	_____	_____
Tiles broken/missing	_____	_____	_____
Tile grout loose/missing	_____	_____	_____
_____	_____	_____	_____
_____	_____	_____	_____
_____	_____	_____	_____

Comments: _____

_____

_____

_____

_____

_____

_____

_____

Ceilings:

	Room	Room	Room
Out of square	_____	_____	_____
Stained/broken/	_____	_____	_____
missing tiles	_____	_____	_____
Light fixture broken/	_____	_____	_____
loose/missing	_____	_____	_____
Grid strips crooked/	_____	_____	_____
bent/wrong	_____	_____	_____
Surface chipped/gouged	_____	_____	_____
Wrong plaster pattern	_____	_____	_____
_____	_____	_____	_____
_____	_____	_____	_____
_____	_____	_____	_____

Comments: _____

_____

_____

_____

_____

_____

_____

_____

Doors and Windows:

	Room	Room	Room
Drapes/curtain/blind/	_____	_____	_____
hardware broken/missing	_____	_____	_____
Window/door not placed/	_____	_____	_____
square/jammed	_____	_____	_____
Hardware broken/missing	_____	_____	_____
Glass broken/uncaulked	_____	_____	_____
Weatherstripping missing	_____	_____	_____
Condensate between panels	_____	_____	_____
Improper swing	_____	_____	_____
_____	_____	_____	_____
_____	_____	_____	_____
_____	_____	_____	_____

Comments: _____

_____

_____

_____

_____

_____

_____

_____

Utilities:

	Room	Room	Room
Electrical receptacle broken/			
missing/wired wrong			
Circuit unenergized			
Light switch broken/			
missing/wrong location			
Diffusers/air returns/			
missing/not flush			
Telephone jack/TV cable/			
missing/wrong location			
Baseboard heater loose			
No hot water			
No cold water			
Security light			
Alarm doesn't work			
Smoke/heat detectors/			
missing or broken			
_____			
_____			

Comments: _____

_____

_____

Kitchen:

	Yes	No	Notations
Appliances work			
Vent hood exhausts			
Dishwasher temp okay			
Counters level/grouted			
Backsplash in place			
Counter height right			
Cabinets fit well			
Doors and drawers work			
GFCI outlets at sink			
Pass through window intact			

Living Room:

	Yes	No	Notations
Ceiling fan work	_____	_____	_____
Thermostat work	_____	_____	_____
Fireplace damper functional	_____	_____	_____
Mantel flush against wall	_____	_____	_____
_____	_____	_____	_____
_____	_____	_____	_____
_____	_____	_____	_____
_____	_____	_____	_____
_____	_____	_____	_____
_____	_____	_____	_____
_____	_____	_____	_____
_____	_____	_____	_____
_____	_____	_____	_____
_____	_____	_____	_____
_____	_____	_____	_____
_____	_____	_____	_____
_____	_____	_____	_____
_____	_____	_____	_____
_____	_____	_____	_____
_____	_____	_____	_____

Dining Room:

	Yes	No	Notations
Chandelier hung	_____	_____	_____
Rheostat works	_____	_____	_____
China cupboard finished	_____	_____	_____
Room exhaust works	_____	_____	_____
_____	_____	_____	_____
_____	_____	_____	_____
_____	_____	_____	_____
_____	_____	_____	_____
_____	_____	_____	_____
_____	_____	_____	_____
_____	_____	_____	_____
_____	_____	_____	_____
_____	_____	_____	_____
_____	_____	_____	_____
_____	_____	_____	_____
_____	_____	_____	_____
_____	_____	_____	_____
_____	_____	_____	_____
_____	_____	_____	_____

Utility Room:

	Yes	No	Notations
Washer hook-ups in			
Dryer outlet work/vent			
Deep sink properly installed			
Linen closets okay			
Water available at taps			
Floor drain drains			
Built-in cupboard okay			

Master Bedroom and Bath:

	Yes	No	Notations
Closet shelving installed	_____	_____	_____
Vanity heights right	_____	_____	_____
GFCI outlets test out	_____	_____	_____
Fixtures drain slow	_____	_____	_____
Ceramic tile grout okay	_____	_____	_____
Countertop level	_____	_____	_____
Fixtures have stop valves	_____	_____	_____
Nonskid tub surface	_____	_____	_____
All accessories built-in	_____	_____	_____
Mixing valves work	_____	_____	_____
Any fixtures leak	_____	_____	_____
Drawers and doors work	_____	_____	_____
Plumbing access door	_____	_____	_____
_____	_____	_____	_____
_____	_____	_____	_____
_____	_____	_____	_____
_____	_____	_____	_____
_____	_____	_____	_____
_____	_____	_____	_____
_____	_____	_____	_____
_____	_____	_____	_____

Second Bedroom and Bath:

	Yes	No	Notations
Closet okay	_____	_____	_____
Vanity right height	_____	_____	_____
GFCI outlets test out	_____	_____	_____
Fixtures work without leaks	_____	_____	_____
Stop valves at fixtures	_____	_____	_____
Tub/shower work	_____	_____	_____
Mixing valves work	_____	_____	_____
Counters level	_____	_____	_____
Drawers and doors work	_____	_____	_____
Accessories built-in	_____	_____	_____
Plumbers access door	_____	_____	_____
Drains drain slow	_____	_____	_____
_____	_____	_____	_____
_____	_____	_____	_____
_____	_____	_____	_____
_____	_____	_____	_____
_____	_____	_____	_____
_____	_____	_____	_____
_____	_____	_____	_____
_____	_____	_____	_____

Third Bedroom and Bath:

	Yes	No	Notations
Closet okay	_____	_____	_____
Vanity right height	_____	_____	_____
GFCI outlets test out	_____	_____	_____
Fixtures work without leaks	_____	_____	_____
Stop valves at fixtures	_____	_____	_____
Tub/shower work	_____	_____	_____
Mixing valves work	_____	_____	_____
Counters level	_____	_____	_____
Drawers and doors work	_____	_____	_____
Accessories built-in	_____	_____	_____
Plumbers access door	_____	_____	_____
Drains drain slow	_____	_____	_____
_____	_____	_____	_____
_____	_____	_____	_____
_____	_____	_____	_____
_____	_____	_____	_____
_____	_____	_____	_____
_____	_____	_____	_____
_____	_____	_____	_____
_____	_____	_____	_____
_____	_____	_____	_____

Garage:

	Yes	No	Notations
Garage doors work	_____	_____	_____
Door to house okay	_____	_____	_____
Outside light works	_____	_____	_____
Concrete floor cracked	_____	_____	_____
Workbench installed	_____	_____	_____
Pegboard up	_____	_____	_____
Crawlspace opening	_____	_____	_____
_____	_____	_____	_____
_____	_____	_____	_____
_____	_____	_____	_____
_____	_____	_____	_____
_____	_____	_____	_____
_____	_____	_____	_____
_____	_____	_____	_____
_____	_____	_____	_____
_____	_____	_____	_____
_____	_____	_____	_____
_____	_____	_____	_____

Basement:

	Yes	No	Notations
Louvre in entry door	_____	_____	_____
Electric panels covered	_____	_____	_____
Circuits labeled	_____	_____	_____
Ductwork insulated	_____	_____	_____
Pipes wrapped	_____	_____	_____
Safety valves tested	_____	_____	_____
Pilot light lit	_____	_____	_____
Furnace/boiler work	_____	_____	_____
Water heater work	_____	_____	_____
Water pressure okay	_____	_____	_____
_____	_____	_____	_____
_____	_____	_____	_____
_____	_____	_____	_____
_____	_____	_____	_____
_____	_____	_____	_____
_____	_____	_____	_____
_____	_____	_____	_____
_____	_____	_____	_____
_____	_____	_____	_____
_____	_____	_____	_____

Other Rooms:

	Yes	No	Notations
_____	_____	_____	_____
_____	_____	_____	_____
_____	_____	_____	_____
_____	_____	_____	_____
_____	_____	_____	_____
_____	_____	_____	_____
_____	_____	_____	_____
_____	_____	_____	_____
_____	_____	_____	_____
_____	_____	_____	_____
_____	_____	_____	_____
_____	_____	_____	_____
_____	_____	_____	_____
_____	_____	_____	_____
_____	_____	_____	_____
_____	_____	_____	_____
_____	_____	_____	_____
_____	_____	_____	_____
_____	_____	_____	_____

Index